Ar-I-Ech and the Spell of Cthulhu

An Informal Guide to Robert E. Howard's Lovecraftian Fiction

Fred Blosser

Pulp Hero Press
The Most Dangerous Books on Earth
www.PulpHeroPress.com

© 2018 Fred Blosser

No part of this publication may be reproduced, distributed, or transmitted in any form or by any means, including photocopying, recording, or other electronic or mechanical methods, without the prior written permission of the publisher, except for brief quotations embodied in critical reviews and certain other non-commercial uses permitted by copyright law.

Although every precaution has been taken to verify the accuracy of the information contained herein, no responsibility is assumed for any errors or omissions, and no liability is assumed for damages that may result from the use of this information.

The views expressed in this book are those of the author and do not necessarily reflect the views of Pulp Hero Press.

Pulp Hero Press publishes its books in a variety of print and electronic formats. Some content that appears in one format may not appear in another.

Editor: Bob McLain
Layout: Artisanal Text

ISBN 978-1-68390-144-0
Printed in the United States of America

Pulp Hero Press | www.PulpHeroPress.com
Address queries to bob@pulpheropress.com

To Donna

CONTENTS

A Note from the Publisher vii

Introduction ix

PART I
Howard, Lovecraft, and the Mythos:
An Overview 1

PART II
Howard's Tales in the Cthulhu Mythos 13

PART III
Howard's Lovecraft-Influenced
Work Outside the Mythos 57

Part IV
Cthulhu and Conan 67

PART V
Howard's Defining Additions
to the Mythos 71

PART VI
Selected Reading List 85

PART VII
Key to Citations 87

APPENDIX A
Kull and the Elder Horrors 89

APPENDIX B
An Argument of Dates in the Life of Solomon Kane, Foe of Demons and Dastards 99

APPENDIX C
Horrors from the Deep: Howard's Stories of Haunted Seaports 105

About the Author *111*

Publisher's Note

Although it might sound like one, "Ar-I-Ech" is not a name pulled from the Cthulhu Mythos. It's how Lovecraft wrote, phonetically, Robert E. Howard's initials, REH. In their extensive correspondence, Howard began his letters to Lovecraft "Dear HPL" and Lovecraft began his letters to Howard "Dear Ar-I-Ech."

Introduction

Born in Texas in 1906, Robert Ervin Howard debuted as a professional writer in 1925 and began to hit his stride in the late 1920s. Overcoming the challenge of isolation from his markets in Chicago and New York, he navigated the popular if often unstable pulp magazine venues of the day as a prolific and versatile storyteller. He worked in genres as diverse as fantasy, adventure, "true" ghost stories, science-fiction, sports, historicals, horror, westerns, pirate, "spicy" titillation, and detective fiction.

With rambunctious stories about the adventures of prizefighters Sailor Steve Costigan, Dennis Dorgan, and Kid Allison, Howard channeled his interest in boxing and employed a flavorful vernacular style reminiscent of Mark Twain, Ring Lardner, and Damon Runyon—the Brooklyn patter of Leo Gorcey crossed with the down-home twang of Slim Pickens.

Influenced by the fiction of Harold Lamb and Talbot Mundy, Howard produced stories of swashbuckling adventure in Middle Eastern and Asian realms, spanning the First Crusade to World War I Arabia. Those settings were strange and exotic to most Americans in his day. Today, post 9-11, the names are all too familiar—Aleppo, Baghdad, Basra, Kabul, Mosul...

Toward the end of his short life, shifting his attention closer to home, Howard displayed a growing interest in the regional history of his native Southwest. He followed this inspiration by embarking on a successful late career of writing humorous westerns for better-paying magazines like *Argosy*. Then in 1936, at age thirty, he committed suicide, cutting short the promise of wider popularity and greater critical recognition.

Although Howard sold to pulps as diverse as *Fight Stories* and *Ghost Stories*, his first, surest, and longest-lasting market was *Weird Tales* magazine. There, readers applauded his fantasy-adventure stories of Solomon Kane, King Kull, Bran Mak

Morn, Turlogh O'Brien, and Conan the Cimmerian. In those years between the two world wars, fantasy and horror were niche genres: Howard's audience was appreciative but relatively small, and checks from *Weird Tales* often were slow in coming. Nevertheless, Howard's specialization in merging sword-slashing action with supernatural fantasy returned immense dividends beyond the brief span of his life. His readers and fellow writers kept alive the memory of his herculean characters through the next two decades, particularly that of Conan, arguably his most colorful and most vividly realized creation.

The known Conan stories were preserved in hardcover in the 1950s by a small publishing house, Gnome Press. Wider exposure came in the 1960s and 1970s, first with paperback publication and then adaptation as a comic-book hero. King Kull, Solomon Kane, and others also returned to print, in mass-market paperback editions, with the tagline "by the creator of Conan." With the 1982 movie *Conan the Barbarian*, Howard's belated reputation as a major architect of twentieth-century popular culture was secured. Along with J.R.R. Tolkien, he now stands as the towering pioneer of the modern heroic-fantasy genre and the forerunner of today's billion-dollar entertainment industry of movies, video and role-playing games, and TV series about wizards, warriors, and imaginary kingdoms.

Beyond his stories of sword-and-sorcery adventure, Howard also wrote prolifically about the supernatural and macabre in modern-day settings. Many of those stories, particularly those from early in his career, employed traditional elements in the vein and sometimes the imitative style of earlier practitioners whom Howard admired.

For example, of the early works, "The Fearsome Touch of Death" (*Weird Tales*, February 1930), in which a man frightens himself to death through an overly active imagination, recalls the psychological irony of Ambrose Bierce's "The Suitable Surroundings" and "The Man and the Snake," and as Howard scholar Rusty Burke has noted, "A Watcher by the Dead." "The Shadow of Doom" (*The Howard Collector* No. 8, Summer 1966) follows the style of Bierce's stories about ghosts and premonitions in mundane surroundings. Howard's approach is earnest and straightforward, notably lacking Bierce's sardonic sting.

Werewolves slink through the related tales "In the Forest of Villefère" (*Weird Tales*, August 1925) and "Wolfshead" (*Weird Tales*, April 1926) in a colorful Renaissance setting that recalls Alexandre Dumas. "The Hyena" locates a similar strain of shape-shifting in an African milieu that recalls Olive Schreiner's 1883 novel *The Story of an African Farm*, which Howard had read. The influence of Sax Rohmer, the creator of Fu Manchu, is evident in the secret cults out of Asia, Africa, and the Middle East in "Skull-Face" (*Weird Tales*, October/November/December 1929).

Some of these are good stories, and "Skull-Face" is notably excellent. But Howard's signature work from 1925 to 1931, in stories where horror rather than exotic adventure predominated, is found in his contributions to the "Cthulhu Mythos." This is the name given to a cycle of tales originated by his contemporary, colleague, and fellow *Weird Tales* mainstay, H.P. Lovecraft, and added to by Howard and diverse other authors who came to comprise what is often referred to as "the Lovecraft Circle."

Howard was one of the first to borrow the names, concepts, and story elements devised by Lovecraft under this overall design, use them in his own stories, and expand them by adding similar inventions of his own. Others did the same, and the conceit continues to draw new fans and contributors, some eighty years after Lovecraft's death.

Howard's ghost, vampire, and werewolf stories only rarely generate critical comment and analysis, in part because so many other writers were substantially more instrumental in shaping those genres. With his additions to the Cthulhu Mythos, Howard himself was a trend-setter as one of the pioneers who developed the basic attributes of the genre, which others have been obliged to follow, use, and emulate. One of the tales, "The Black Stone," is widely ranked among Howard's best; I would argue that others deserve similar recognition.

This informal guide briefly reviews the background of Howard's Cthulhu fiction, summarizes and discusses the stories that he contributed to the cycle, surveys associated stories by Howard that were influenced by Lovecraft's style or themes even though not strictly part of the Cthulhu Mythos, briefly addresses the relationship between Conan and Cthulhu, and catalogs Howard's defining additions to the Mythos: people, places, books, and things.

To simplify the citations to Howard's Cthulhu- and Lovecraft-influenced stories, I've added a key based on acronyms for the titles of the stories (for example, "BN" = "The Black Stone"). The key appears at the end of this guide, with a listing of the books that I have used for sources; in each citation, the reader is directed to the source book by page number. I've also appended, as the next-to-final section, a selected reading list to direct curious readers' attention to some other resources about the topic of Howard and Cthulhu.

As always, anyone writing about Robert E. Howard must acknowledge the signal achievements of the late Glenn Lord (1931–2011) in preserving and promoting Howard's legacy. Marcelo Anciano, Jack and Barbara Baum, Rusty Burke, George T. Hamilton, Paul Herman, Don Herron, Patrice Louinet, Joe Marek, Dennis McHaney, Rob Roehm, Damon Sasser, and Roy Thomas, to name those who come immediately to mind, have continued the mission to promote the commercial availability of Howard's work and to champion wider critical appreciation.

PART I
Howard, Lovecraft, and the Mythos: An Overview

Whence come these fears from the outside? Surely in its infancy, mankind faced beings that live today only in dim ancestral memories, forgotten entirely by the material mind. Otherwise, why is it we half visualize in that other, subconscious mind, perhaps, shapes beyond the power of man to describe?
—Robert E. Howard to H.P. Lovecraft, ca. 1930; *Robert E. Howard: Selected Letters, 1923–1930*.

Tales of Cthulhu

H.P. Lovecraft (1890–1937) once said: "[A]ll my tales are based on the fundamental premise that common human laws and interests and emotions have no validity or significance in the vast cosmos-at-large" (H.P. Lovecraft, *Selected Letters II, 1925–1929*, ed. August Derleth and Donald Wandrei: Arkham House, 1968, p. 150). In the late 1920s, with "The Call of Cthulhu" (*Weird Tales*, February 1928) and "The Dunwich Horror" (*Weird Tales*, April 1929), this perspective began to inform a gradually coalescing cycle of related stories in which Lovecraft imagined human existence as "a placid island of ignorance in the midst of black seas of infinity" (H.P. Lovecraft, "The Call of Cthulhu," in *The Call of Cthulhu and Other Weird Stories*, ed. S.T. Joshi: Penguin Books, 1999, p. 139). In Lovecraft's vivid fancy, our tiny harbor of refuge is surrounded and occasionally invaded by trans-stellar and trans-dimensional forces almost beyond the capacity of humans to perceive and understand.

Certain elements were common to this nascent concept, sometimes drawn from earlier and otherwise unrelated stories by Lovecraft. His cosmically powerful forces were often embodied as, or associated with, grotesque avatars or servitors, which were fearfully worshipped as "gods" by cultists because of their immense power and unearthly nature. Many bore names meant to replicate inhuman vocalizations, such as Cthulhu, Yog-Sothoth, and Azathoth. Some names reflected known nomenclature, such as Dagon and Hydra, suggesting that some entities of the Mythos entered or influenced ancient Mediterranean and Middle Eastern mythologies. In some instances, the entities were so cryptic or alien that they were known simply as the Old Ones or the Great Old Ones.

In Lovecraft's imagining, this dreadful pantheon was memorialized in forbidden books of suppressed knowledge, the most prominent of which was the *Necronomicon* by "the mad Arab Abdul Alhazred." These tomes provided incantations and occult formulas by which Cthulhu and others could be summoned from outer space, other dimensions, or remote places on earth, with dire results for humankind.

Some of the stories were set in Lovecraft's native Providence, Rhode Island; others were laid in the fictitious town of Arkham, Massachusetts; and others in the squalid, likewise imaginary Massachusetts backwaters of Dunwich and Innsmouth. Lovecraft intermingled his fictitious details with references to actual places, people, belief systems, historical events, and mystic volumes of lore, creating a powerful illusion of verisimilitude.

Other writers congregated around Lovecraft. With his cordial approval, they began to borrow his concepts, creatures, and gothic prose style for their own fiction, mostly published in *Weird Tales* and similar pulp magazines. These fantasists included, early on, Robert Bloch, August Derleth, Henry Kuttner, Frank Belknap Long, Clark Ashton Smith, and Donald Wandrei, in addition to Robert E. Howard.

Long knew and socialized with Lovecraft personally. The others lived long distances away, and some were still in their teens. They struck and maintained friendships with Lovecraft through regular exchanges of letters in that era before

Facebook, Skype, fantasy conventions, direct dialing, on-line forums, and cheap airfares made more personal interaction affordable, even possible, on modest incomes.

Over time, this accruing school of weird fantasy became known as the Cthulhu Mythos. Lovecraft himself never referred to it as such, and never fully developed it as a systematically organized concept. The closest he came to applying a label was to humorously call it "Cthulhuism and Yog-Sothothery" (S.T. Joshi, *H.P. Lovecraft: A Life:* Necronomicon Press, 1996, p. 402).

Howard Comes to the Mythos

Howard's association with Lovecraft began in July 1930, when he wrote their mutual editor, Farnsworth Wright, to praise a reprint of his older contemporary's novelette, "The Rats in the Walls," in the June 1930 *Weird Tales*. Lovecraft, he said, "must have the most unusual and wonderfully constructed brain of any man in the world. He alone can paint pictures in shadows and make them terrifically real" (Robert E. Howard to H.P. Lovecraft, ca. 1930; *Robert E. Howard: Selected Letters, 1923-1930*, ed. Glenn Lord, with Rusty Burke and S.T. Joshi: West Warwick, RI: Necronomicon Press, 1989, p. 48; hereafter cited as *SL 1923-1930*).

Although "The Rats in the Walls" lies outside the Cthulhu cycle, it is distinguished by other features of style and plot that must have impressed Howard. Related in dark, dense prose, it tells the story of an American who has taken up residence in the gloomy ancestral manor of his forebears in Britain, and what happens when his family's ancient legacy of degeneracy and cannibalism reasserts itself. During this period, Howard was fascinated by the obscure corners of ancient British history, the same material that serves as a backdrop for Lovecraft's gruesome story.

The letter to Wright was followed immediately by an exchange of correspondence with Lovecraft himself, initiating a long-distance friendship by post that continued until Howard's death in 1936. From the formal salutation "Dear Mr. Lovecraft" at the outset, Howard eventually transitioned to a more relaxed "Dear HPL," while Lovecraft headed his letters with "Dear REH" or sometimes "Dear Ar-I-E'ch." The latter address was consistent with Lovecraft's practice of bestowing phonetically spelled and vaguely ominous nicknames on his correspondents, once they had established a mutual rapport.

In an early letter, Howard swapped what he knew about early Celtic Britain with what Lovecraft knew, and discovered that Lovecraft shared his appreciation for the Welsh horror writer Arthur Machen, whom Howard had pastiched in a then-unpublished story, "The Little People," in 1928. He also asked Lovecraft for information about Cthulhu, the *Necronomicon*, and so forth, with the unspoken question of whether these were items of actual, esoteric lore that Lovecraft had tapped into from a formal knowledge of the occult. Lovecraft clarified ("much to my chagrin," Howard commented to another friend) that those concepts were simply "figments of his own imagination," and had not been lifted from any pre-existing body of esoteric belief (*SL 1923-1930*, p. 57).

In turn, Howard noted that a reader had asked in the letter column of *Weird Tales* whether Kathulos of Atlantis, the villain of Howard's fantasy serial "Skull-Face" (*Weird Tales*, October-November-December 1929), had been inspired by Lovecraft's monstrous Cthulhu, introduced the year before in "The Call of Cthulhu." "[I]n reality I merely manufactured the name at random, not being aware at the time of any legendary character named Cthulhu—if indeed there is," Howard told Lovecraft (*SL 1923-1930*, p. 56).

One wonders whether Howard was exercising selective memory, or whether there was an unconscious influence that he may not himself have realized. Similarities exist between Cthulhu and Kathulos that go beyond the mere fact of two names that sound alike. Like Cthulhu, Howard's character returns to the modern world after a long suspended animation under the sea. Both Cthulhu and Kathulos are venerated by primitive, suppressed cults that have waited for their resurrection. Still, in style and plot, the two stories are quite different, and one character is reasonably human while the other isn't. It doesn't seem to be an issue on which Howard would deliberately wish to mislead Lovecraft, especially in a letter filled with praise for "one whose works I so highly admire."

An Outpouring of Cosmic Horror

Once they had become acquainted by mail, Howard and Lovecraft began to cross-pollinate each other's fiction. Howard wrote several stories that reference Lovecraft's creations by name, and others that mimic his prose style and themes without overtly invoking the Cthulhu mythology. For his part, Lovecraft retroactively incorporated some concepts from Howard's earlier fiction into the catalog of Mythos lore.

Kathulos of Atlantis from "Skull-Face" was recast by Lovecraft as "L'mur Kathulos" in "The Whisperer in Darkness" (*Weird Tales*, August 1931); the same story referenced "Bran," a nod to Howard's concept of a secret, modern-day cult that venerates the ancient Pictish king Bran Mak Morn from Howard's sword-and-sorcery work. In "The Shadow Out of Time" (*Astounding Stories*, June 1936), the prehistoric Serpent Men from the King Kull story "The Shadow Kingdom" (*Weird Tales*, August 1929) are name-checked as "the reptile people of fabled Valusia."

With Lovecraft as a model, Howard commenced to write about recklessly curious seekers of forbidden wisdom who endeavor to traffic with "nameless shapes...in the dark places of the world" (BN 171). In those works, he referenced Cthulhu and Yog-Sothoth, devised his own additions to the cycle, most significantly a loathsome nineteenth-century German tome, *Nameless Cults*, and juxtaposed those creations with allusions to actual books, belief systems, and historical events in the manner of Lovecraft.

Lovecraft obliged by citing *Nameless Cults* in his fiction alongside his own *Necronomicon* and similar imaginary volumes by Bloch, Derleth, and others, notably in "The Dreams in the Witch House" (*Weird Tales*, July 1933), "The Haunter of the Dark" (*Weird Tales*, September 1935), and "The Thing on the Doorstep" (*Weird Tales*, January 1937). In those tales, he referred to the book as *Unaussprelichen Kulten,* a title devised by Derleth and given Lovecraft's imprimatur (H.P. Lovecraft, *Selected Letters IV, 1932–1934*, Arkham House, 1976, p. 401). Howard himself only used the Derleth-devised German title once, in an unfinished story.

This immersion in Lovecraftian style would follow a pattern that Howard replicated time and again in his career: a compulsive fascination with a given author, character, theme, or setting; a burst of creativity in writing about the subject; and then a tapering off as he lost interest, focus, or a secure market, and moved on to a new enthusiasm.

Three stories are clearly identifiable as Lovecraft-inspired from this period of mid- to late-1930, based on their content, dates of publication, and references in Howard's letters. They are "The Children of the Night," "The Black Stone," and "The Thing on the Roof." Possibly around this same time, Howard rewrote "John Grimlan's Debt," an unsold deal-with-the-devil weirdie from 1929, to add Cthulhu references, and changed the title to "Dig Me No Grave."

From similar internal evidence, two uncompleted Howard stories are likely to have been started during this time but set aside: "Dagon Manor" and "The House." Of these, "The House" is a substantial addition to the canon, even in unfinished form and irrespective of material added by August Derleth in completing the fragment years later. Derleth published the completed version as "The House in the Oaks."

Howard's entry into the Lovecraft circle is notable as an early step in formalizing the Cthulhu Mythos and creating around Lovecraft's fiction a "shared universe" of concepts and characters, as modern publishers would phrase it. The stories theretofore contributed by Frank Belknap Long, Donald Wandrei, and Clark Ashton Smith were constructed around Lovecraft's general themes of cosmic horrors and mythic "gods," but they rarely used Lovecraft's nomenclature, as S.T. Joshi has observed (Joshi, *H.P. Lovecraft: A Life*, p. 546. See also "Notes Toward a History of the Cthulhu Mythos," compiled by David E. Schultz (*Crypt of Cthulhu* No. 92, Eastertide 1996).

As far as I'm aware, "The Children of the Night" was the first published story ever, by a fantasist other than Lovecraft, to incorporate Cthulhu and Yog-Sothoth by name. The apparent exception would seem to be "The Electric Executioner" by Adolph de Castro (*Weird Tales*, August 1930), which contained the variant names "Cthulhutl" and "Yog-Sototl," along with "R'lyeh" from "The Call of Cthulhu" (Adolph de Castro, "The

Electric Executioner," in H.P. Lovecraft, *The Horror in the Museum and Other Revisions*, Arkham House, corrected third printing, 1989, p. 74). However, the Cthulhu allusions are actually Lovecraft's; he revised a manuscript by de Castro and added the names "for sheer fun" (*SL 1923–1930*, p. 57). Ironically, this was a point of confusion for Howard before he became acquainted with Lovecraft, wondering whether there was a common pool of occult mythology from which two different writers had drawn (*SL 1923–1930*, pp. 56-57).

During the same period of work in mid- to late 1930, in a stunning display of creativity and versatility, Howard also contributed prizefighting tales to *Fight Stories* and *Action Stories*, and rounded out his Solomon Kane and Turlogh O'Brien heroic fantasy series with valedictory works that overlapped the Cthulhu stories. I consider the Turlogh O'Brien story, "The Gods of Bal-Sagoth," to be part of the Cthulhu cycle for reasons that I discuss later in the guide. The Solomon Kane story, "The Footfalls Within" (*Weird Tales*, September 1931), I've included as an associated story if not formally part of the Mythos.

Howard also began to write thundering historical novelettes about the centuries-long clash between European chivalry and the legions of Genghis Khan, Saladin, Tamerlane, Suleiman, and other medieval conquerors in the Middle East and Central Asia. These historicals, for which Howard found a steady if not always unfailing market in the pulp first called *Oriental Stories* and then rebooted as *Magic Carpet*, are some of his most vivid and deeply felt works.

Recession and Epilogue

Going into 1931, Howard maintained his prolific correspondence with Lovecraft and followed the Cthulhu fiction of Lovecraft and others: for example, in a circa June 1931 letter, praising Frank Belknap Long's "The Horror from the Hills," which appeared in the January-February and March-April 1931 issues of *Weird Tales* (*Robert E. Howard: Selected Letters 1931–1936*, ed. Glenn Lord with Rusty Burke, S.T. Joshi, and Steve Behrends: Necronomicon Press, 1991, p. 4; hereafter cited as *SL 1931–1936*). But he was beginning to turn to other genres and in the process gave less attention to the Mythos, at least in terms of concentrating on stories that added directly and substantially to the lore. As other Lovecraft correspondents such as Bloch, Derleth, and Kuttner stepped up to further expand the Mythos, Howard stepped back.

Observers have advanced plausible explanations for this shift. Other enthusiasms had seized his attention, initially with the emergence of *Oriental Stories* and its promise of a commercial venue for historical fiction. Howard keenly enjoyed dramatizing history, particularly medieval history during the clashes of Eastern and Western armies in the Holy Land and points east. If he had multiple markets for historical adventure, Howard said to a friend, he'd "never write anything else" (*SL 1931-1936*, p. 11). Then, as his sports markets folded in 1932, new ventures claimed Howard's time and concentration, partly from the need to regain his financial footing by diversifying. These new directions included the debut of Conan; experiments in detective, pirate, and "spicy" fiction; adventure stories set in the Middle East and Central Asia in modern times; and a fascination with U.S. Southwestern and Southern themes.

The latter preoccupation, in particular, consumed more and more of Howard's attention in the final years of his life. Ironically, this interest had been sharpened by his correspondence with Lovecraft. In his long letters, Howard increasingly had written about the history and culture of the Southwest and the South as Lovecraft replied with information about his native New England. Among other ways in which this interest shaped the course of Howard's fiction after 1933, it gave rise to three memorable horror fantasies with regional settings: "Black Canaan" (*Weird Tales*, June 1936), "The Dead Remember" (*Argosy*, August 15, 1936), and "Pigeons from Hell" (*Weird Tales*, May 1938). But the shadows that brood over these tales are those of voodoo curses and bayou magic, not Cthulhu and *Nameless Cults*.

Another plausible theory offered for the sputtering out of Howard's Lovecraft-flavored stories: that Howard may have felt constrained by the typical formula of the Cthulhu story, in which the narrator customarily faints, runs away hysterically, or passively awaits his doom when encountering the Old Ones or their avatars. This convention bumped up against Howard's taste for stories driven by aggressive heroes who do not shy away from conflict. On the contrary, they race into battle, usually against overwhelming odds.

As Lovecraft himself said admiringly, "He was, above everything else, a lover of the simpler, older world of barbarian and pioneer days...when a hardy, fearless race battled and bled, and asked no quarter from hostile nature" (H.P. Lovecraft, "In Memoriam: Robert Ervin Howard," *Miscellaneous Writings*, ed. S.T. Joshi: Arkham House, 1995, p. 125).

There was a financial disincentive, too. The market for Cthulhu fiction was limited to *Weird Tales*, a relatively low-paying, often late-paying outlet. Editor Farnsworth Wright usually bought Howard's submissions, especially after Howard became a favorite with readers, but did not always do so. Once Howard was over his first flush of enthusiasm, and had invested his best ideas in three or four stories, he had no commercial motivation to put further time and effort into writing a type of story that did not draw on his natural instincts, and further, one with a limited potential for generating fresh plots.

Still, fantasy and horror were fundamental interests, and he never altogether abandoned the Cthulhu school or themes and elements suggestive of it. For its own part, the Mythos continued to expand after Howard departed, as Lovecraft's younger friends Bloch and Kuttner started their careers in *Weird Tales* in the mid-1930s. Derleth began to put the "gods" of the Mythos into a systematic framework in his stories of the early 1940s, with results that are debated by Lovecraft fans today. Derleth also preserved the Mythos and other tales of Lovecraft, Howard, and the *Weird Tales* school in hardcover editions through his pioneering press, Arkham House, founded with Donald Wandrei.

Lovecraft and Howard continued to correspond until Howard's death in 1936. The sense of personal and professional loss expressed by Lovecraft in a eulogy for Howard published in *Fantasy Magazine*, September 1936, is palpable: "It is hard to describe precisely what made Mr. Howard's stories stand out so sharply; but the real secret is that he himself is in every one of them..." ("In Memoriam: Robert Ervin Howard," p. 125).

Lovecraft himself died in 1937—like his friend Howard, at a far-too-early age. Two of his final Mythos stories, "At the Mountains of Madness" (*Astounding Stories*, February-April 1936) and "The Shadow out of Time" (*Astounding Stories*, June 1936), put a stronger science-fictional spin on the Cthulhu entities, more Arthur C. Clarke than Edgar Allan Poe. *Weird Tales* succumbed in 1954. Through the 1950s, the Mythos to a great extent owed its survival to August Derleth, who continued sporadically to write new Cthulhu stories and to preserve the old in ongoing Arkham House editions.

With a younger generation's revival of interest in classic fantasy in the 1960s, Cthulhu and Yog-Sothoth experienced a resurgence. New writers including Ramsey Campbell, Brian Lumley, and Colin Wilson added fresh stories to the Mythos, followed more recently in the high-tech era by Donald R. Burleson, Peter Cannon, C.J. Henderson, W.H. Pugmire, and others. Hollywood discovered Lovecraft, beginning with Roger Corman's *The Haunted Palace* (1963) and Daniel Haller's *Die, Monster, Die!* (1965) and *The Dunwich Horror* (1970). This would probably have pleased Robert E. Howard, who was a movie fan, although he like other Lovecraft enthusiasts might have had mixed feelings about the cinematic results.

Along with this renaissance in the Cthulhu Mythos and growing commercial recognition of Lovecraft, S.T. Joshi, Maurice Lévy, Dirk W. Mosig, Robert M. Price, and others have led insightful scholarship on Lovecraft and his work. Volumes of Lovecraft and new Mythos tales by contemporary writers crowd the shelves in both virtual and brick-and-mortar book stores today, and the name and image of Cthulhu are ubiquitous in our popular culture. Thanks to mass media and the Internet, Cthulhu is known to millions of people who probably have never read a Lovecraft story.

What Is Cthulhu and What Isn't?

Critics and observers differ in their lists of Howard's Cthulhu stories. No two lists name all the same titles. Jack L. Chalker's "Howard Phillips Lovecraft: A Bibliography" in *The Dark Brotherhood and Other Pieces*, edited by August Derleth

(Arkham House, 1966, p. 233), enumerates only four stories and the minor poem "Arkham." At the other extreme, *Nameless Cults: The Cthulhu Mythos Fiction of Robert E. Howard*, edited by Robert M. Price (Chaosium Press, 2001), collects 13 Howard stories, four tales completed by others from Howard fragments, and "The Challenge from Beyond," a collaborative 1935 novelette by Howard, Lovecraft, Long, A. Merritt, and C.L. Moore. But no poem. Lin Carter, Charles Hoffman and Marc Cerasini, Ben Solon, and others who have surveyed or listed Howard's Mythos stories are equally diverse in their selections.

Two factors may be responsible. First, some lists predate the great era of Howard popularity in the 1970s, when much previously unpublished material by Howard first saw print. For example, "The Hoofed Thing," a Cthulhu story by any measure, was first published in *Weirdbook* in 1970 (under the title "Usurp the Night"), a few years after the works by Chalker and Solon.

The second factor is a question of criteria: there are no generally agreed-upon guidelines for determining if a given story by Howard is a Cthulhu Mythos work. "The Black Stone" and "The Thing on the Roof" consistently are included. Other tales make one list but not another. Some observers count "The Shadow Kingdom" and "Skull-Face" because those stories include names that Lovecraft added to his evolving scheme after their original publication. Others observers do not, presumably because in those instances, Howard had not set out intentionally to expand Lovecraft's lore. In my opinion, there is no inherently "right" or "wrong" list of Howard's Cthulhu stories, as long as the reasons for inclusion or omission are clear.

In this informal study, I have established my own standards. In the next two sections, I note and discuss the stories that I consider, respectively, to be 1) Howard's contributions to the Cthulhu cycle and 2) the associated stories that display a strong Lovecraft influence, even if the classic names of the Mythos are absent.

PART II
Howard's Tales in the Cthulhu Mythos

I've used two criteria in ranking a story by Robert E. Howard as part of the Cthulhu Mythos. I have made that determination for those works in which Howard deliberately set out to pastiche Lovecraft, referred to the "gods" and books invented by Lovecraft and added his own, and introduced characters who have entered the fabric of the Mythos through incorporation by Lovecraft and other writers. The stories that align with this category are "The Children of the Night," "The Black Stone," "The Thing on the Roof," "The Fire of Asshurbanipal," "Dig Me No Grave," "Untitled Fragment" ("Beneath the glare of the sun…"), "The Hoofed Thing," and "The House" in its unfinished, pure-text Howard form. The first three are closely related tales that provide the foundation for Howard's work in the Cthulhu cycle.

As a second criterion, I have included a story if it inherently shares a theme or characters with any in the first list and includes any reference to any Cthulhu name, or simply if it includes a Cthulhuvian reference. The four stories in that category are "The Gods of Bal-Sagoth," "People of the Dark," "Worms of the Earth," "Black John's Vengeance," and one fragment, "Dagon Manor."

"The Children of the Night"
First published in Weird Tales, April–May 1931

Plot
Irish-American John O'Donnel, the scholar Conrad (no first name given), and their friends are gathered socially at Conrad's home in England to discuss various topics of mutual interest, including the mystery of the Little People, the mysterious race that lay behind the "troll and dwarf legends" of Western Europe and the British Isles. As a diminutive Neolithic axe of mysterious origin is passed around, O'Donnel is struck on the head and regresses into a distant past life as Aryara, a primitive hunter in Bronze Age Britain. Falling asleep on watch, Aryara had allowed his fellow tribesmen to be massacred by the Children of the Night, also known as the Little People: a race of human lineage with "deformed dwarfish bodies, yellow skin, and hideous faces." O'Donnel relives Aryara's subsequent death in battle with the killers, then regains consciousness again in the present to realize that Ketrick, one of his acquaintances, is the modern descendant of his ancient enemies. As the story ends, he determines to kill Ketrick to expiate the shame incurred by Aryara thousands of years before.

Discussion
"The Children of the Night" was Howard's freshman venture into Lovecraft's "Cthulhuism," containing his first-ever references to *Nameless Cults* and Von Junzt. It name-checks Cthulhu, Yog-Sothoth, and Clark Ashton Smith's Tsathoggua, the latter possibly because Lovecraft noted Smith's contribution of that entity in one of his early letters to Howard. The story mentions the *Necronomicon*, and follows Lovecraft's pattern of interweaving real and imaginary mythology and bibliography. It observes these conventions so deftly that an unassuming lay-reader may have difficulty in separating the real from the unreal, and in teasing out Howard's inventions from Lovecraft's, as when one of the characters says that Howard's Von Junzt "was one of the few men...who could read [Lovecraft's]...*Necronomicon* in the original Greek translation" (CN 220).

An entity devised by Howard, Gol-goroth, is cataloged with Cthulhu, Yog-Sothoth, and Clark Ashton Smith's Tsathoggua, whom Lovecraft had already inducted into the coalescing Mythos. Gol-goroth appears in the heroic fantasy "The Gods of Bal-Sagoth" (*Weird Tales*, October 1931) as a "huge formless thing" (GS 337) worshipped in a lost city, but otherwise was unused by Howard. On the bookshelf in Conrad's library, the fictitious *Nameless Cults* incongruously sits side-by-side with first editions of two very real gothic novels, Horace Walpole's *The Castle of Otranto* (1764) and the Marquis de Grosse's *Horrid Mysteries* (1796).

By inference, Conrad alludes to Cthulhu as a fictitious character with modern origins in the weird-fantasy fiction genre when he cites "The Call of Cthulhu" as "one of the three master horror-tales" (CN 219). At the same time, Cthulhu has a "real" existence in Conrad's world as one of the "nameless and ghastly gods and entities" worshipped by obscure, age-old cults. This same conceit of the Cthulhu entities existing simultaneously as pulp magazine fiction and as objects of worship by actual cults would occur again in later Mythos tales by other writers. In August Derleth's "Beyond the Threshold," for example (*Weird Tales*, September 1941), *The Outsider and Others*—the pioneering 1939 collection of Lovecraft stories from Arkham House, edited by Derleth and Donald Wandrei—serves the protagonists equally as well as the *Necronomicon* does in unlocking the mysteries of the Cthulhu entities.

The Cthulhu-linked mythology alluded to in "The Children of the Night" and its two loosely connected sequels, "People of the Dark" and "Worms of the Earth," won a high accolade by Lovecraft in a playful "genealogy" described in an April 27, 1933, letter to his friend James F. Morton. There, Lovecraft traces his own fanciful ancestry to "Ghoth the Burrower, one of the Little People" (that is, one of the Children of the Night) from a union with Viburnia, presumably a Romano-British woman; one of Ghoth's progenitors in turn was Cthulhu (H.P. Lovecraft, *Selected Letters IV, 1932–1934*, ed. August Derleth and James Turner: Arkham House, 1976, p. 183).

"The Children of the Night" generally has had a mixed reception, although Lovecraft apparently liked it (*SL 1931–1936*, p.

5) and it placed among "stories ranking second" in the *O. Henry Memorial Award: Prize Stories of 1931* (*SL 1931–1936*, p. 43). Two characters in the story seem to be projections of Howard's own personality and wish-fantasies. Conrad enjoys a dual reputation as a commercially affluent author of "swashbuckling novels" and as a transgressive artiste who edits *The Cloven Hoof*, "a poetry magazine whose contents had often aroused the shocked interest of the conservative critics" (CN 220). O'Donnel is a thinker who enjoys intellectual companionship, but also a hate-driven man of action in his past incarnation as Aryara and in his present, twentieth-century skin once he learns Ketrick's true nature.

The long, opening section of the story, set in Conrad's "bizarrely fashioned study," establishes the basic premise of the plot: "nightmare cults" from antiquity continue to exist "in the dark corners of the world today" (CN 217, 220). With this concept, Howard knits together three otherwise disparate fantasy elements. One is the cult worship of Cthulhu and other shadowy entities. The second is a cult revolving around the legacy of an ancient king of the enigmatic Picts of Britain and Scotland, Bran Mak Morn. The third is the mystery of the Little People, a concept that Howard had already used in a then-unpublished 1928 fantasy, "The Little People," without any tie-in with Cthulhu. Now, with "The Children of the Night," he rethought his initial vision of the Little People, incorporated his revised design into the Mythos, and began to explore it more systematically.

By the time "The Children of the Night" was published, *Weird Tales* readers were already familiar with Bran Mak Morn from "Kings of the Night" in the November 1930 issue, a heroic fantasy set in Roman Britain that showcased Bran as the leader of a native uprising against the Romans, aided by the mystic return of King Kull from ages past. In that story, Bran embodied Howard's ideal of a physically powerful, charismatic hero: brooding but fearless and shrewd, and ruthless when necessary in pursuit of a greater good—"a born king of men" (Howard, "Kings of the Night," in *Bran Mak Morn: The Last King*, ed. Rusty Burke: Ballantine Books/Del Rey, 2005, p. 73). The Picts were portrayed ambiguously but mostly sympathetically as a waning culture in a last-ditch resistance against the fascistic might of the invading Roman Empire. In "The Children of the Night," Howard suggested a more sinister aspect of the Picts as "a revival of an older, darker empire dating back into the Stone Age" (CN 221). He offered a vaguely creepy incarnation of Bran as an object of cult worship by descendants of the Picts, who make a pilgrimage to a "great, nameless cavern" where they worship a stone image of Bran. Like Cthulhu and the skull-faced Kathulos of Atlantis, Bran is gone but not forgotten, and his return is anticipated by a fervid cult. Clemants, another of Conrad's guests, says Bran's votaries are secretly "waiting for the stone image of the great Bran to breathe and move with sudden life, and come from the great cavern to rebuild their lost empire."

These allusions are clear to readers today, who have access to works that were unavailable to the readers of "The Children of the Night." "Men of the Shadows," submitted by Howard to *Weird Tales* in 1926 but rejected, relates the history and prehistory of the Picts at length, amplifying the passing reference to "an older, darker empire" in "The Children of the Night." It finally saw publication in 1969. I might note, parenthetically, that "Kings of the Night" was not the only crossover story between the Kull and Bran series. "Men of the Shadows" alludes to Kull's inhuman enemies, the Serpent Men, and suggests that remnants of their cult survived beyond Kull's age into Bran's—but no further. "The power of the Serpent is broken. The neophytes offer up no more humans to their dark divinities," Bran exults ("Men of the Shadows," in *Bran Mak Morn, The Last King*, p. 18).

The stone image of Bran is prominent in "The Dark Man," which followed in the December 1931 issue. In that tale of Howard's Irish hero Turlogh O'Brien, a Pict of the eleventh century says, "A wizard made this statue while the great Morni yet lived and reigned, and when he died in the last great battle, his spirit entered into it. It is our god" ("The Dark Man," in *Bran Mak Morn, The Last King*, p. 162). When one is aware of these other stories, there is less disparity between the concept of Bran in "Kings of the Night" and that in "The Children of the Night."

The element of the Children of the Night flows from Howard's inaugural correspondence with Lovecraft. Howard had already read the Welsh horror writer Arthur Machen (1863-1947), who in "The Shining Pyramid" (1895) and other stories, imagined that the early Indo-Europeans had been preceded into Western Europe and the British Isles by a migration of "prehistoric Turanian inhabitants...who were cave dwellers" ("The Shining Pyramid" in *Tales of Horror and the Supernatural*: Pinnacle Books, 1971, p.177). Those stunted, debased troglodytes were encountered by the first Indo-Europeans, and memorialized in later ages in legends of "the Little People"—malicious trolls, dwarves, and elves.

According to Machen's biographer, Wesley Sweetser, the Welsh writer's "concept of fairies as dwarfed and cannibalistic creatures" may have derived from the Celtic studies of a nineteenth-century scholar, Sir John Rhŷs (see Wesley Sweetser, *Arthur Machen*: Grosset & Dunlap, 1964, p. 118). "Turanian" is an obsolete term from nineteenth-century anthropology, which theorized an ancient migratory culture of mixed Caucasian and Asian or "Mongoloid" genetics. To Rhŷs' theories, Machen added the notion that remnants of these noxious Little People survive in modern times in remote areas of Britain, practicing grisly rituals. Mindful of Victorian conventions, Machen was circumspect in describing their practices. His vague description of one rite, "the voice of a woman cried out loud in a shrill scream of utter anguish and terror" (*Tales of Horror and the Supernatural*, p. 171), suggests that they involved the abduction, rape, and human sacrifice of young women.

Howard had pastiched Machen in "The Little People," a story written in 1928 but unpublished during Howard's lifetime. In that story, he conflated Machen's "Turanian" race with his own evolving concept of the Picts. The protagonist of "The Little People" explicitly alludes to Machen's "The Shining Pyramid" as "a masterpiece of outré literature" (Robert E. Howard, "The Little People," in *Bran Mak Morn, the Last King*, p. 199). After their initial exchange of letters in which the two writers discussed Machen, Howard thanked Lovecraft for information which led him to reconsider his earlier concept. Now he was predisposed to distinguish the Little People from the Picts as separate waves of immigrants to Britain: "I readily see the truth of your remarks that a Mongoloid race must have been responsible for the myths of the Little People" (Robert E. Howard to H.P. Lovecraft, ca. August 1930; *Robert E. Howard: Selected Letters, 1923–1930*, p. 53; West Warwick, RI: Necronomicon Press, 1989).

In "The Little People," Howard had described the Little People as a culture "known variously as Turanians, Picts, Mediterranean, and Garlic-eaters" (*Bran Mak Morn, the Last King*, p. 199). In "The Children of the Night," he adapts the terminology "Mongoloid" suggested by Lovecraft. This change is signaled in a conversation between Conrad and another character, Taverel. Taverel interprets Von Junzt in *Nameless Cults* as suggesting that the Mediterraneans or Picts were "the first settlers [of Scotland]…who gave rise to the tales of earth spirits and goblins." But he is challenged (or corrected) by Conrad, who instead proposes that "the Mediterraneans were preceded by a Mongoloid type, very low in the scale of development" (CN 221).

Another shout-out occurs when Conrad cites Machen's "The Novel of the Black Seal" as one of "the three master horror-tales": the other two are "The Call of Cthulhu" and Edgar Allan Poe's "The Fall of the House of Usher" (CN 219). There isn't any Poe to speak of in "The Children of the Night" (unless one sees a comparison between Conrad's almost suffocatingly gothic home and the house of Roderick Usher), but there's plenty of Lovecraft and Machen: "The Novel of the Black Seal" is another of Machen's stories about the Little People. This juxtaposition of Lovecraft and Machen further suggests that the concepts of the Cthulhu cult and the Little People were intertwined in Howard's fancy. Soon after starting the correspondence with Lovecraft, Howard expressed interest in getting Machen's address in England and writing to him. Nothing seems to have come of this, but it's interesting to think what may have transpired if Howard had pursued the notion (*SL 1923–1930*, p. 60).

Two details of the Little People mythology that appear prominently in "The Novel of the Black Seal" also turn up in "The Children of the Night." Machen's character Professor

Gregg speaks of a "primitive stone axe" that he finds "utterly unmanageable" when he handles it: "whether there is some peculiar balance, some nice adjustment of weights, which require incessant practice,or whether an effectual blow can be struck only by a certain trick of the muscles, I do not know" (Arthur Machen, "The Novel of the Black Seal," in *The White People and Other Weird Stories*, ed. S.T. Joshi: Penguin Books, 2011, pp. 59, 60). Compare the axe in "The Children of the Night," the balance of which is "off center." Conrad's guest Taverel says he would have to "adjust all of my mechanics of poise and equilibrium to handle it" (CN 222).

A rural youth in the Machen story, Jervase Cradock, has "something of the blood of the 'Little People'" (*The White People and Other Weird Stories*, p. 64) as the child of a woman apparently impregnated in a rape by the creatures on a lonely country road at night (here again the reader has to make the assumption because Machen never explicitly says this was the case). Jervase has a "strange sibilance" in his voice, like the hissing of the phonograph [needle]" (p. 45). His counterpart in Howard's story is Ketrick, with "a slight and occasional lisping of speech" (CN 218), a genetic heritage from the "hissing, reptilian speech" of the Children of the Night (CN 223).

O'Donnel speculates that remnants of the Little People persisted into historical times in Wales as "survivals" from Aryara's time, and that Ketrick, like Jervase, descends from an ancestral rape of a Welsh woman by one of the Little People (CN 231). Ketrick's eyes that "seemed to slant," suggesting "a reversion of type to some dim and distant ancestor of Mongolian blood" (CN 218), echoes Machen's reference to the "marked Mongolian character" of the eyes of the Little People in "The Shining Pyramid" (Machen, *Tales of Horror and the Supernatural*, p. 175).

Howard's references to "royal Aryan" lineage of his blond prehistoric hero, standing in counterpoint to the degraded Children of the Night "with their deformed dwarfish bodies, yellow skin, and hideous faces" (CN 231, 225), may be disturbing to modern readers who come to the story unaware of controversies in recent decades over racial attitudes in Howard's fiction, drawn from now-discredited anthropological theories of the nineteenth and early twentieth centuries. Howard scholars have widely agreed that it's preferable to let his stories stand in their pure-text form, and to air such issues for honest analysis, rather than to expurgate or censor as some editors did with various Howard stories in the 1960s and 1970s.

Beyond the Little People, "The Novel of the Black Seal" contains another element that seems to have stimulated Howard's imagination, "a lump of black stone" that Machen's character Professor Gregg associates with the Little People (*The White People and Other Weird Stories*, p. 35). That element isn't reflected in "The Children of the Night," but it would emerge as the centerpiece of his next contribution to the Cthulhu cycle and as a feature in two subsequent Cthulhu-linked fantasies.

Yet another influence colors "The Children of the Night," unrelated to Lovecraft or Machen. The theme of past-life regression was suggested by Jack London's novel *The Star Rover* (1915), in which a convict confined in a strait-jacket in San Quentin Penitentiary explores a succession of earlier incarnations, including an existence in the Bronze Age in which the god Il-marinen was worshipped, as he is by Aryara's people in "The Children of the Night." Howard told his friend Harold Preece in a 1930 letter that he had "read and re-read" London's novel "for years" (Robert E. Howard, "Letter to Harold Preece," in *The Conan Swordbook*, ed. L. Sprague de Camp and George Scithers: The Mirage Press, 1969, p. 5).

This seemingly uneven confluence of moody, gothic horror out of Lovecraft and Machen, with a brief interlude of primitive carnage suggestive of London, may account for a critical opinion by the late L. Sprague de Camp and his co-authors that "The Children of the Night" was "perhaps the least well-conceived of all the stories Howard sold in his lifetime" (L. Sprague de Camp, Catherine Crook de Camp, and Jane Whittington Griffin, *Dark Valley Destiny: The Life of Robert E. Howard*: Bluejay Books Inc., 1983, p. 260). If that was the intended point of the comment, I would argue the contrary. The influences are well-integrated, the segment set in the Bronze Age is integral to the plot, and the combination gives the story a flavor unique to Howard.

"The Gods of Bal-Sagoth"

First published in Weird Tales, *October 1931*

Plot

Captured by Vikings, Turlogh O'Brien, an outcast Irish warrior of the early eleventh century, is shipwrecked on an unknown Caribbean island with the Saxon pirate Athelstane. They encounter Brunhild, Norse by birth, who had made herself the queen of the lost city of Bal-Sagoth, only to be overthrown by the high priest Gothan. They return to the city and Brunhild regains the throne with the two warriors' help. But Gothan, priest of the dark god Gol-goroth, marshals his grisly powers and kidnaps the queen for sacrifice. Athelstane slays the dark god (or its avatar), which in turn kills Gothan before it dies, but a massive stone idol of Gol-goroth falls on and crushes Brunhild. Bal-Sagoth collapses in civil chaos, and then the indigenous warriors of the surrounding islands (apparently Taino or Carib Indians) invade to complete the slaughter. Turlogh and Athelstane are rescued by a passing Castilian warship.

Discussion

Only mentioned by name in passing in "The Children of the Night," the entity Gol-goroth figures more prominently in "The Gods of Bal-Sagoth." He is "the god of darkness who sits forever in the Temple of Shadows" in the lost city of Bal-Sagoth, where he is worshipped with sacrificial rites by the priest Gothan and his acolytes (GS 320).

An avatar or issue of Gol-goroth appears in the story as a "great black shape" with "flaming eyes," standing "man-like, upon two tree-like legs," but its features are "not of a man, beast or devil" (GS 335–336). When the creature is slain by Athelstane the Saxon, the action underscores the principle stated in a later story, "The Hoofed Thing," that an entity is "vulnerable to material weapons" if it is made of flesh or assumes fleshly form on the earthly plane. A gigantic statue of Gol-goroth is "sinister and abhorrent," but not otherwise described (GS 337).

The late Lin Carter proposed to induct into the Mythos another horror from "The Gods of Bal-Sagoth." This was Groth-golka, a twelve-foot-high, predatory, apparently flightless bird with "wicked red eyes and cruel curved beak" (GS 313). Turlogh and Athelstane meet Brunhild when they save her from the monster. Carter suggested that the creature slain by the castaways was an "avatar" of a Cthulhuoid entity (see Lin Carter, "The Fishers from Outside," in *The Xothic Legend: The Complete Mythos Fiction of Lin Carter*, Chaosium Books, 1997, p. 181). Howard implies that Groth-golka was terrestrial, the last survivor of a species, of whom the priests of Bal-Sagoth "made a god" (GS 317). Of all things, the beast may remind older readers of an uglier version of the aggressive, overgrown baby chick created and animated by Ray Harryhausen in the 1961 movie, *The Mysterious Island*.

Since Howard never referred to Groth-golka in any other story, and seems not to have included him in the pantheon of cosmic Old Ones with Cthulhu and Gol-goroth, I've chosen not to list him as one of Howard's defining additions to the Mythos. Carter fans may feel free to disagree.

"The Black Stone"
First published in Weird Tales, *November 1931*

Plot
The narrator (unnamed) becomes curious when he reads about a mysterious monolith, the Black Stone, in *Nameless Cults*. Therein it is referred to as "one of the keys" ((BN 154). Traveling to the remote Hungarian village of Streigocavar, he locates the Black Stone, "octagonal in shape, some sixteen feet in height and about a foot and a half thick. ... [H]ammers had done little more than to flake off small bits of stone and mutilate the characters which once had evidently marched in a spiraling line round and round the shaft to the top" (BN 159–160). The narrator learns that the village stands on the site of an earlier, aboriginal settlement called Xuthltan. Before its utter obliteration by invading Turks in 1526, Xuthltan had been the home of a bestial cult that summoned a "strange deity" through violent rites on Midsummer Night. Dozing near the stone on that appointed night, the narrator witnesses an orgiastic ceremony of short, skin-clad primitives "whose features were

degraded as from a mixture of some baser, alien strain I could not classify" (BN 164). In the vision, he sees a priest whip a young woman and sacrifice an infant, at which a "toad-like *thing*...bloated, repulsive, and unstable" materializes atop the monolith, waiting "lustfully and slobberingly" as the priest hands the woman to him (BN 166, 167). A dream? The narrator finds further evidence a few days later, excavating an old manuscript which records that the Turks slew a "monstrous, wallowing, toad-like being" during their sweep through Hungary in the sixteenth century. With the manuscript, the narrator finds a repulsive image of the monster. He realizes that somehow he had witnessed a ghostly ceremony from millennia past, and that the Black Stone is a key to "abhorrent spheres" of supernatural existence. He wonders, "Man was not always master of the earth—*and is he now?*" (BN 171)

Discussion

"The Black Stone" is one of Howard's most popular stories— perhaps his most often reprinted, with some seventy appearances in collections and anthologies since its original 1931 publication. It was included in the memorial Howard volume edited by August Derleth for Arkham House in 1946, *Skull-Face and Others*, and in *Crimson Shadows: The Best of Robert E. Howard, Volume One*, edited by Rusty Burke (Ballantine Books/Del Rey, 2007; Subterranean Press, 2009). It appears in August Derleth's seminal anthology *Tales of the Cthulhu Mythos* as part of a selection "representative of the host [of fantasies] written for the Mythos" by Lovecraft's admirers (Derleth, "The Cthulhu Mythos," in *Tales of the Cthulhu Mythos*, ed. August Derleth: Arkham House, 1969, p. xii).

As fans have observed, the story is richly (or some would say chokingly) laden with Lovecraftian rhetoric: "a mysterious, intangible rustling and whispering was abroad" (BN 162) ... "something snapped in my brain and I fell into a merciful faint" (BN 167) ... "my blood chilled in my veins, my hair stood up and my tongue cleaved to my mouth" (BN 169) ... "ghastly murmurings and stealthy treadings of ghoulish horrors" (BN 169) ... "tittering obscene gloating of evil over the souls of men" (BN 169).

The plot is transparently modeled on that of "The Call of Cthulhu." A scholar happens across something that mystifies him: in the case of Howard's unnamed protagonist, Von Junzt's reference to the Black Stone as a "key"; for Lovecraft's narrator Thurston, a bas-relief statue of Cthulhu. Each man investigates further, gathering a collection of arcane, bewildering information that initially raises more questions than it answers. Eventually (to borrow the title of a much later Mythos story by Brian Lumley), an item of supporting evidence turns up, allowing the narrator to make sense of what he has pulled together from disparate sources. Thurston locates a manuscript by a deceased sailor which documents the emergence of Cthulhu from the Pacific. Howard's narrator finds the Turkish manuscript and the grotesque image that make clear the nature of the Black Stone.

There is a clever if not necessarily intentional reversal in the two plots. The image of Cthulhu is one of several enigmatic items compiled by Thurston, meaningless in and of itself. The image of the monster found by the narrator of "The Black Stone" is the critical piece of the puzzle that enables him to make sense of everything else at hand, and corroborates the theory he had begun to formulate.

The story elaborates on the history of Von Junzt and *Nameless Cults* only briefly sketched in "The Children of the Night." Born in 1795, Von Junzt was found dead in 1840 in "a locked and bolted chamber...with the marks of taloned fingers on his throat" (BN 154). In addition to the original German edition of his book, there were inferior editions in the United States and Great Britain. For the first time, we hear of "the mad poet" Justin Geoffrey, who wrote the "weird and fantastic" *The People of the Monolith*, "while traveling in Hungary," and later "died screaming in a madhouse" (BN 155, 157). An "excerpt" from Geoffrey's poem appears as an epigraph at the beginning of the story. (More information on these defining additions to the Mythos is in Part V of this guide.)

The Black Stone reflects concepts from both Lovecraft and Machen. Presumably, Howard derived his conceit of an inscribed Black Stone from a black stone in Professor Gregg's possession in "The Novel of the Black Seal," which is etched with characters "four thousand years old at least. Perhaps much more." The characters scratched into this stone, also called the Black Seal, the Sixtystone, Ixaxar, and Ishakshar, are the written symbols that correspond to the "ghastly jargon" of the Little People's spoken language (Machen, *The White People and Other Weird Stories*, p. 64). The Black Seal opens the door of contact with the secret world of the Little People, just as the Black Stone of Xuthltan opens the door to the "abhorrent spheres" spoken of by Howard's narrator. (Actually, two black stones appear in Machen's story; the second is inscribed with both the glyphs of the Little People and cuneiform, enabling Gregg to translate the primitive written language of the Little People.)

Two allusions in "The Black Stone" provide further points of crossover linking Machen, "The Children of the Night," and "The Black Stone." In the latter story, the narrator finds a passage in another obscure tome (Otto Dostmann's *Remnant of Lost Empires*) which states that the inscriptions on the Black Stone of Xuthltan are "unmistakably Mongoloid" (BN 155). This is connective tissue with Machen's description of the "Mongolian" shape of the eye as a characteristic among the Little People (Machen, *Tales of Horror and the Supernatural*, p. 161), and also with Conrad's reference in "The Children of the Night" to the "Mongoloid type."

Howard's narrator describes the ancient folk who worship at the Black Stone of Xuthltan: "some have Slavic features, but others are "degraded as from a mixture of some baser, alien strain." They are "a shorter, more squat race, whose brows were lower, whose faces were broader and duller" (BN 164). This reference to "duller," perhaps signifying diminished intellectual capacity, recalls the description of Jerase Craddock in "The Novel of the Black Seal" as being "of weak intellect" (Machen, *The White People and Other Weird Stories*, p. 62). The narrator's informants in Stregoicavar believe that "the sturdy, original Magyar-Slavic stock had mixed and intermarried with a degraded aboriginal race until the breeds had blended, producing an unsavory amalgamation" (BN 158-159).

The story doesn't explicitly say that this "degraded race" and the Little People are one and the same, but it's a reasonable assumption to make. The practice by the folk of Xuthltan in offering sacrifices to their god from "the girls and babies stolen from...the lower valleys" (BN 162) recalls the grisly ceremony of the Shining Pyramid described in Machen's story of that name. Machen's Black Seal differs from Howard's Black Stone in one significant respect. The Black Seal is "about two inches long, and something like an old-fashioned tobacco-stopper, much enlarged" (Machen, *The White People and Other Weird Stories*, p. 36). So, it is significantly smaller than Howard's tall monolithic slab. But Lovecraft makes up the difference. Two monoliths in "The Call of Cthulhu" offer models for this aspect of the Black Stone.

In Chapter II of Lovecraft's novelette, police raid a ceremony of cultists in a Louisiana swamp and find "a great granite monolith some eight feet in height," around which a "hybrid spawn were braying, bellowing, and writhing" (H.P. Lovecraft, "The Call of Cthulhu," in *The Call of Cthulhu and Other Weird Stories*, ed. S.T. Joshi: Penguin Books, 1999, p.152). This is much like the "blind passion of bestiality" (BN 166) witnessed by Howard's narrator in the ritual at the Black Stone. In "The Call of Cthulhu," a "noxious" idol of Cthulhu sits on top of the Louisiana monolith (Lovecraft, *The Call of Cthulhu and Other Weird Stories*, p. 152). Similarly, but involving a direct rather than symbolic presence of the entity being worshipped, atop Howard's squats a living monstrosity, "a huge monstrous toad-like *thing*" (BN 166).

The sexual element of frenzied worship is more blatant in Howard's story. The devotees at the Black Stone shout in "slobbering ecstasy" as a bestial priest, "from whose waist hung a goatskin, and whose features were entirely hidden by a sort of mask from a huge wolf's head," flogs the naked female sacrifice-to-be "incessantly" with fir switches. The young woman eventually falls "quivering and panting," to plant "fierce hot kisses" on the Black Stone (BN 165, 166). The intimations of sexual sadism, orgasm, and oral phallicism are plain to read, especially since earlier in the story, Howard had said that the people of the Black Stone "had been members of that fertility cult which once threatened to undermine European civilization and gave rise to the tales of witchcraft" (BN 161).

This line of thought seems to have been stimulated by conversations in Howard's and Lovecraft's letters about primitive phallic worship and the historical origins of the witchcraft myth. "A wealth of fiction could be written about [a presumed medieval witchcraft cult]—especially about the time that European civilization seemed on the verge of crumbling before its insidious undermining," Howard wrote (*SL 1923–1930*, p. 68). And later (December 1930), "Why should the [witchcraft] cult be merely a fertility worship? Why should it not have deeper, darker significance, dating from pre-human memories? In fiction, at least!" (*SL 1923–1930*, p. 77). Or in "The Black Stone," at least. The detail of the infernal priest flogging the intended female sacrifice with switches, severely enough that she leaves "a heavy track of blood" from her injuries (BN 166), would have been strong stuff for younger *Weird Tales* readers in the 1930s. Modern readers may find it equally unsettling, given today's heightened sensitivity about violence toward women, whether in popular media or in real life.

The second model from Lovecraft for the structure of the Black Stone occurs in Chapter III of "The Call of Cthulhu." There, a "hideous monolith-crowned citadel" is pushed up seismically from the Pacific, on top of a structure "whereon Cthulhu was buried" (Lovecraft, *The Call of Cthulhu and Other Weird Stories*, p. 165). Lovecraft's narrator Thurston fears that the mass was only the pinnacle of a colossally larger structure that remained underwater, the citadel or vault of R'lyeh. "When I think of the *extent* of all that may be brooding down there I almost wish to kill myself forthwith" (Lovecraft, *The Call of Cthulhu and Other Weird Stories*, p. 165). Likewise, Howard's narrator theorizes that the Black Stone is only the "spire on a cyclopean black castle" still buried under the Hungarian mountains: "May no man ever seek to uproot the ghastly spire..." (BN 171).

Howard also follows Lovecraft's lead with his easily rattled protagonist, who "[falls] into a merciful faint" as the monster with its "lust, abysmal greed, obscene cruelty, and monstrous evil" is about to receive his bloody, naked female sacrifice (BN 167).

At the same time that the correspondence with Lovecraft had stimulated Howard's interest in Cthulhu, the debut of *Oriental Stories* had fueled his drive to write about the sword-shattering clashes of Eastern and Western armies on the medieval frontiers of Europe and the Mediterranean. The Turkish invasion of 1526, alluded to in "The Black Stone," would later take front stage as the setting for Howard's superlative historical adventure "The Shadow of the Vulture," published in *Magic Carpet*, the successor to *Oriental Stories*, in January 1934.

If a more robust market for Howard's sword-and-sorcery had existed in the early 1930s, might he have been tempted to write a sequel in which the heroes of "The Shadow of the Vulture," Gottfried von Kalmbach and Red Sonya of Rogatino, are swept into sixteenth-century Stregiocavar by the invading Turks, and join with them to slay the "ghastly thing" on the Black Stone? It's an interesting, teasing thought.

"The Thing on the Roof"
First published in Weird Tales, *February 1932*

Plot

The narrator, an unnamed anthropologist, is surprised when his rival Tussmann seeks his help in locating a copy of *Nameless Cults* in its original edition. He obliges, and Tussmann finds the information he needs: a reference to an ancient temple in the jungles of Central America, and a mummy around whose neck hangs a toad-shaped jewel. Von Junzt hints that the jewel is a "key" to a treasure below the temple. Tussmann goes to Central America and on his return, asks the narrator to come to his estate in Sussex and bring Von Junzt's Black Book with him. There, Tussmann says vaguely that he found the temple and a crypt beneath, and the jewel from the mummy, but nothing else that he could "bring away." Now reading *Nameless Cults* again, he finds a passage warning the curious not to disturb "sleeping things." From upstairs comes a noise like the stamping of hooves on the roof of Tussmann's house. Left alone, the narrator finds a passage in Von Junzt about "a huge, tittering, tentacled, hoofed monstrosity" worshipped beneath the "Temple of the Toad" by a pre-Indian people in Central America. The entity is their "treasure." Hearing a crash upstairs and sounds of tittering and squishing inside

Tussmann's room, the narrator breaks open the locked door. The toad-shaped jewel is gone, the room reeks of a nauseating stench, and Tussmann lies dead on the floor, "the print of an enormous hoof" on the remains of his crushed face.

Discussion

Each of the three foundational Cthulhu stories by Howard—"The Children of the Night," "The Black Stone," and "The Thing on the Roof"—reiterates and elaborates upon at least one concept from the tale that immediately preceded it. "The Black Stone" fleshed out the slender references to Von Junzt and his dreadful book from "The Children of the Night." In turn, "The Thing on the Roof" takes up a detail offered in passing in "The Black Stone," where the narrator correlates the inscriptions on the Black Stone with "crude scratches on a gigantic and strangely symmetrical rock in a lost valley of Yucatan."

"The Thing on the Roof" then refers back to the earlier story when Tussmann says that inscriptions on the copper chain affixed to the toad-shaped jewel from Central America have a "faint resemblance" to "certain partly defaced hieroglyphics on a monolith known as the Black Stone in the mountains of Hungary" (TR 166). The enigmatic concept of a "key" recurs, this time a jewel in the "repulsive" form of a toad instead of a stony monolith.

Another "excerpt" from Justin Geoffrey heads the story ("They lumber through the night..."), not from *The People of the Monolith* but from another shuddersome poem, *Out of the Old Land* (TR 162). The tale also offers additional details about expurgations and omissions from the later American and British editions of the Black Book. (The history of *Nameless Cults* is further outlined in a later section of this informal guide.)

In finding the citations from Von Junzt that Tussmann needs, the narrator is helped by "Professor James Clement of Richmond, Virginia"—evidently not the same "Clemants" mentioned in "The Children of the Night" as one of Conrad's visitors, despite the similarity of names. One wonders if the reference to Richmond was occasioned by Howard's appreciation for Poe, whom he named as one of his favorite writers, although he didn't rate him as highly as he rated Lovecraft and Machen (*SL 1923–1930*, p. 49).

As in Lovecraft's "The Dunwich Horror," where a quotation from the *Necronomicon* says that "[a]s a foulness shall ye know Them"—the Yog-Sothoth entities, that is (H.P. Lovecraft, "The Dunwich Horror," in *The Dunwich Horror and Others*, corrected ninth printing, Arkham House, 1992, p. 170)—Howard's unseen hoofed monster brings with it a characteristically "foul and overpowering stench" (TR 170). The protagonist goes to investigate the climactic racket in Tussmann's locked room with "shattered nerves," but he shows a little stronger fiber than the typical Lovecraft character. He doesn't faint when he sees the "red ruin of [Tussmann's] skull and face"; at least, if he does, his narration happens to omit that detail (TR 170).

Howard was particularly proud of the story: "not only the best story by far that I ever wrote, but…in my honest opinion a really first-class weird story judged by any standards." But it had a difficult road to publication. Howard reported that it was rejected by *Weird Tales* editor Farnsworth Wright as "too erudite for the general reader," then also rejected by two other markets. "Then Farnsworth asked to see it again," and that time accepted it, Howard said (*SL 1930–1936*, p. 10). Lovecraft's verdict: "I know it's trite, but something in it gave me a kick for all that. Maybe it was von Junzt & the Black Book" (see David E. Schultz, "Notes Toward a History of the Cthulhu Mythos," *Crypt of Cthulhu* No. 92, Eastertide 1996, p. 18).

In divorcing the narrator from Tussmann's backstory on the Yucatan Peninsula and keeping the horror from the temple unseen at the end, except for the horrific result of its visit, Howard seems to be applying a principle that he advanced in a letter to Lovecraft around September 1930: "The fault I find with so many so-called horror tales (particularly including my own) is that the object of horror too swiftly becomes too solid and concrete. … When a writer specifically describes the object of his horror, gives it worldly dimensions and solid shape, he robs it of half its terrors" (*SL 1931–1936*, p. 64). It may be a matter of taste whether "The Thing on the Roof" is more frightening than Howard's other Cthulhu stories, in which the monsters appear on stage. At least we can give Howard credit for a noble experiment.

Solon called the story "typical Cthulhu Mythos" (Ben Solon, "Howard's Cthuloid Tales," in *The Conan Swordbook*, ed. L. Sprague de Camp and George Scithers: The Mirage Press, 1969, p. 77). Hoffman and Cerasini similarly judged it as "standard Cthulhu Mythos fare" (Charles Hoffman and Marc Cerasini, "The Strange Case of Robert Ervin Howard," in *The Horror of It All*, ed. Robert M. Price: The Borgo Press, 1990, p. 95). Dennis Rickard judged "The Black Stone" to be "the most noteworthy" of Howard's Cthulhu stories, but "The Thing on the Roof" as "[m]uch less satisfying" (Dennis Rickard, "Through Black Boughs: The Supernatural in Howard's Fiction," in *The Dark Barbarian*, ed. Don Herron: Greenwood Press, 1984, pp. 73, 74).

August Derleth included "The Thing on the Roof" in the second Arkham House collection of Howard stories, *The Dark Man and Others* (1963), the contents of which, he said, were "on the whole, secondary to the work to be found in the memorial omnibus," *Skull-Face* ("Introduction," *The Dark Man and Others*: Arkham House, 1963, p.viii). Robert M. Price rated the tale rather more favorably as "number two behind 'The Black Stone' among Howard's best efforts at Mythos fiction" ("Introduction," *Tales of the Lovecraft Mythos*, ed. Robert M. Price: Fedogan & Bremer, 1992, p. xviii). Howard probably would be pleased that the story has been reprinted some 51 times.

"People of the Dark"

First published in Strange Tales of Mystery and Terror, *June 1932*

Plot

Irish-American John O'Brien intends to kill Englishman Richard Brent, his rival for the affection of Eleanor Bland. Coming to Dagon's Cave for that purpose, he slips on a flight of tiny stone steps in the cavern and, unconscious, remembers a past life as Conan of the Reavers, a Gaelic pirate in the early Iron Age. In this former existence, he tries to abduct a beautiful Celtic tribeswoman, Tamera, on a raid, but she and her sweetheart Vertorix flee into Dagon's Cave. Conan pursues, and he rescues Vertorix and Tamera from the stunted, debased troglodytes who lurk in the cave, the Children of the Night. Separated from them in their escape, Conan watches from a ledge as the two Celts jump to their death from the opposite cliff to escape their loathsome pursuers. Recovering consciousness in the present, O'Brien realizes that Vertorix and Tamera were previous incarnations of Brent and Eleanor, and that he owes a debt for the wrong that Conan inflicted on them. O'Brien watches tragedy begin to replay itself, when he observes from a ledge as Brent and Eleanor emerge on the opposite cliff, to be attacked by a serpentine monster, the last mutated remnant of the Children of the Night. With the gun that he had planned to use to kill Brent, O'Brien instead dispatches the monster.

Discussion

"People of the Dark" (sometimes reprinted as "The People of the Dark") replays the theme of "The Children of the Night" in its story of a modern man who is given the opportunity to redress an ancient wrong. The title beings are the descendants of the Children of the Night from the earlier story, even further debased and less human than their ancestors. Howard even calls them "the Children of the Night" throughout the tale; "people of the dark" appears only in the title. A Black Stone figures into the plot, resembling both the Black Seal of Arthur Machen's horror stories and the monolithic Black Stone of Howard's Von Junzt tale. Venerated by the People of the Dark, it is a "cryptic black object, carven with mysterious hieroglyphics." Howard includes an imaginative suggestion that the stone once "stood in that grim circle of monoliths called Stonehenge" (PD 153).

The dense, brooding mood and style of the "The Children of the Night" story are absent, replaced by more action and a conventional love story. Although Howard doesn't mention Von Junzt or *Nameless Cults*, the name "Dagon's Cave" refers to the Cthulhu entity Dagon, invented by Lovecraft in "Dagon" (*Weird Tales*, October 1923) and "The Shadow over Innsmouth" (*Weird Tales*, January 1942, but written in 1931 and first published as a chapbook by fan publisher William Crawford in 1936). How Dagon bears upon the mythology of the Little People, which Howard continues with this story, isn't made clear; in some stories such as this, Howard seems to have enjoyed the process of invoking the Cthulhu mythology for its sinister implications, leaving the reader to speculate, for example, on the existence of a Dagon cult in ancient Britain.

As Howard followers such as Rusty Burke and Patrice Louinet have noted, this Conan of the historical Iron Age clearly shows Howard's imagination at work in moving toward the amalgamation of influences and characteristics that shortly would lead to the birth of Conan of Cimmeria.

"Worms of the Earth"
First published in Weird Tales, *November 1932*

Plot
Bran Mak Morn, the king of the Picts, enraged by the tyrannical occupation of Britain by the Romans, schemes to use occult forces against the enemy. In return for Bran's "fierce kisses" and sexual favors, the witch Atla discloses the location of the Black Stone, the "one thing sacred" to the "worms of the earth," otherwise known as the Children of the Night. Stealing the Stone, Bran pledges to return it if the creatures undermine the Roman stronghold, the Tower of Trajan. They do so with results that horrify even Bran. Keeping his promise, he meets with Atla and the creatures by night, returning the Stone by dashing it into the midst of the troglodytes, and flees in revulsion.

Discussion
In addition to continuing the mythology of the Little People begun in earnest as an adjunct to the Cthulhu cycle in "The Children of the Night," this story from the Bran Mak Morn saga delivers a steady litany of Cthulhu references: "Black gods of R'lyeh, even you would I invoke. ... I swear by the Nameless Ones..." (WE 90), Bran rants. Atla invokes "the black secrets of R'lyeh" (WE 115). Place names include Dagon-moor, Dagon's Barrow, Dagon's Ring, and Dagon's Mere, further interlinking Cthulhu with the Children of the Night cycle. The Black Stone is "a solid sullen block of darkness" with "cryptic characters carved thereon." The references to Dagon as part of four place names are as mysterious as the reference in "People of the Dark."

So, too, the mention of "R'lyeh," which in Lovecraft's fiction was the undersea city in which Cthulhu slept. A draft of "Worms of the Earth," published in 2001 in hardcover and 2005 in trade paperback, contains an even more direct reference to the greatest Old One, as Bran swears instead by "the bones of Cthulhu" (WE 253).

The story discloses what happens when someone comes face to face with unspeakable Lovecraftian horrors. The Roman governor whom Bran makes a target of the Worms of the Earth emerges with "the blank glassy eyes, the bloodless features, the loose, writhing, froth-covered lips of sheer lunacy" (WE 123–124). It suggests that the Howard and Lovecraft protagonists who flee from the horrors of the Cthulhu deities are wise to do so.

"The Fire of Asshurbanipal"
First published in Weird Tales, *December 1936*

Plot

American Steve Clarney and his Afghan partner Yar Ali seek the lost city of Kara-Shehr, the City of Evil, in the Arabian desert. Legend has it that the ruins hold a fabulous treasure, a gem called the Fire of Asshurbanipal. They find the city and the gem, clutched in the hand of an ancient skeleton, but they are attacked and overcome by outlaws led by an old enemy, Nureddin el Mekru. Nureddin takes the gem, disregarding an old man in his band who says that the stone is cursed and that it has a demonic custodian. As the outlaw seizes the gem, a hidden door in the wall opens, and a tentacle emerges and seizes Nureddin, pulling him inside. Tied up on the floor, Steve and Yar Ali see the door open again, a pair of "monstrous eyes" burning in the darkness. They close their eyes as coldness and a foul smell fill the air. Steve opens his eyes, catches a glimpse of something going back behind the door and shutting it, and passes out. A set of splayed, taloned prints is visible in the dust on the floor. The Fire of Asshurbanipal is back in the skeleton's grip, and on the floor, Nureddin's severed head.

Discussion

There are two versions of "The Fire of Asshurbanipal," one better known and more frequently anthologized than the other, and neither published during Howard's lifetime. The less-often-reprinted version includes a passing reference to "the ancient City of Evil spoken of in the *Necronomicon* of the mad Alhazred," but incorporates no overtly supernatural elements. In that iteration, Nureddin reaches for the gem, dislodges the skull of the skeleton, and is fatally bitten by an adder coiled inside the skull. It was published long after Howard's death in *The Howard Collector* for Spring 1972.

The other, better-known version was submitted to *Weird Tales* by Howard's father shortly after his son's death, and published in the December 1936 issue with a stunning cover illustration from the story, by the great fantasy artist J. Allen St. John. That version retains the reference to the *Necronomicon* and Alhazred (FA 20), and proceeds to significantly dial up the Cthulhu content. As Nureddin prepares to take the Fire of Asshurbanipal from the skeleton, an aged Bedouin in his gang warns him fearfully not to do so, as in the time of Asshurbanipal, the seventh-century BCE king of Assyria, a magician named Xuthltan "dared the horrors of a nameless vast cavern in a dark, untraveled land," put a spell on the demon that guarded a fabulous gem "carved of the frozen flames of Hell," and brought the jewel to the king's court (FA 36).

Presently, to retain the gem, Xuthltan fled to Kara-Shehr, but there the ruling potentate ordered him to be put to death. Dying, the sorcerer "cr[ied] out on the forgotten gods, Cthulhu and Koth and Yog-Sothoth, and all the pre-Adamite Dwellers in the black cities under the sea and the caverns of the earth." He cursed the king to sit on his throne, holding the jewel, "until the thunder of Judgment Day." Then "came a grisly shape which stretched forth fearsome paws and laid them on the king, who shriveled and died at their touch" (FA 37-38). The old man warns that the demon still watches over the jewel and will horribly kill anyone who tries to steal it—as events soon bear out.

The presentation of the monster hovers about midway between the strategy employed in "The Thing on the Roof"— where the entity that kills Tussmann never appears on stage—and the full disclosure of the monster in "The Black Stone." Steve Clarney mostly keeps his eyes shut when the guardian comes into the ruined throne room. However, as the creature returns to its hiding place after emerging with Nureddin's severed head, Steve sneaks a glance:

"It was gigantic and black and shadowy; it was a hulking monstrosity that walked upright like a man, but it was like a toad, too, and it was winged and tentacled. I saw only its back; if I'd seen the front of it—its face—I'd have undoubtedly lost my mind" (FA 44).

The sight is so frightening that Steve responds more as a typical Lovecraft protagonist would react than as a typical, seen-it-all Howard hero would. He faints.

A "deadly cold" follows the entity, and its breath is "soul-shakingly foul" (FA 40). The latter detail calls to mind the "quotation" from the *Necronomicon* that appears in "The Dunwich Horror": "As a foulness shall ye know Them" (Lovecraft, *The Dunwich Horror and Others*, p. 170)—that is, the Old Ones—and also the vile smell left by the monster in "The Thing on the Roof."

Steve Clarney refers to the creature in passing as "an elemental demon out of the earth" (FA 43). Later, controversially, August Derleth would refer to the Cthulhu entities as "elementals" in "The Return of Hastur" (*Weird Tales*, March 1939), "Beyond the Threshold" (*Weird Tales*, September 1941), and other stories. In Derleth's usage, each Cthulhu entity corresponds to a particular physical element of air, water, earth, or fire. "Nyarlathotep corresponds to an earth-elemental, Cthulhu to a water-elemental...", begins one litany by Derleth (*Tales of the Cthulhu Mythos*, p. viii). For critical perspectives on Derleth's practice, see *H.P. Lovecraft: A Life* by S.T. Joshi: Necronomicon Press, 1996, pp. 638–640, and *A Look Behind the Derleth Mythos: Origins of the Cthulhu Mythos* by John D. Haefele: H. Harksen Productions, 2012, pp. 232–236).

Howard doesn't repeat the term "elemental" in any of his other Cthulhu stories, and its appearance in "The Fire of Asshurbanipal" seems only to refer to the stark, basic evil of the entity, and not to any intentional association with the physical elements as Derleth proposed in his stories.

Like "The Black Stone," the *Weird Tales* version of "The Fire of Asshurbanipal" was included in the memorial volume, *Skull-Face & Others*. It's an unusual but effective combination of fast-action adventure with Cthulhu fantasy that reads like a sword-and-sorcery tale in modern dress.

"Dig Me No Grave"
First published in Weird Tales, *February 1937*

Plot
Kirowan is awakened in the dead of night by his friend John Conrad, and the two men proceed to the house of John Grimlan, a recluse who died an hour before. Conrad asks Kirowan's help in carrying out Grimlan's instructions about the disposition of his body, including the command, "Dig me no grave; I shall not need one." The "evil and perverse" recluse had a dark reputation among the local townspeople, who believed that he had sold his soul to the devil, and that his epileptic seizures were a sign of demonic possession. Conrad attests to the dead man's interest in "the darker, grimmer phases" of the occult, and remarks that Grimlan once implied that he was much older than he appeared to be. In Grimlan's "great grim house perched like a bird of evil" on a hillside, Conrad and Kirowan find the occultist's corpse laid out on a table, covered by a silken robe, and surrounded by seven black candles. An enigmatic stranger with Asian features, already in the room, suggests they begin the ceremony dictated in Grimlan's instructions. As Conrad recites the bizarre contents of Grimlan's testament, Kirowan pieces together a story about the occultist's journey to the "black citadels of Koth," and a deal there with the "Darke lord" by which he was granted two hundred and fifty additional years of life in return for delivering his body and soul to the Prince of Darkness upon his death. A groan comes from the corpse, the candles go out, and Conrad and Kirowan flee. As the house goes up in flames behind them, they see rising from it a gigantic, bat-like shadow, carrying "a small, white thing, like the body of a man."

Discussion

Like "The Fire of Asshurbanipal," "Dig Me No Grave" was sent by Howard's father to *Weird Tales* shortly after his son's death. In an invaluable essay archived on the internet, "Grief & Greed: Isaac Mordecai Howard and the Robert E. Howard Estate, June 1936 to March 1937," Howard scholar Patrice Louinet discusses the history of the story, originally titled "John Grimlan's Debt" and in its original form submitted unsuccessfully to *Ghost Stories* in 1929. Like the Cthulhu tales previously discussed, it has enjoyed a robust reprinting history in some forty collections and anthologies in the U.S. and abroad. In the 1963 jacket art for *The Dark Man and Others* from Arkham House, artist Frank Utpatel depicted the final scene of the story, as the demonic bat rises from the burning house with Grimlan's body.

The mythological background of the story combines plentiful Cthulhu references with allusions to other belief systems, real and fictitious. "What do you know of Yog-Sothoth, of Kathulos and the sunken cities?" Grimlan asks in a conversation recalled by Conrad. "None of these names is even included in your mythologies. Not even in your dreams have you glimpsed the black cyclopean walls of Koth, or shriveled before the noxious winds that blow from Yuggoth" (DG 248). Among other occurrences, "Yuggoth" appears in Lovecraft's sonnet cycle "Fungi from Yuggoth," which Howard read around August 1930 (*SL 1923–1930*, p. 53), and in Lovecraft's "The Whisperer in Darkness," where it is identified with the then newly discovered dwarf planet Pluto. Howard's reference to "Kathulos and the sunken cities" recalls the backdrop of his novella "Skull-Face," and also Lovecraft's incorporation of "L'mur-Kathulos" into the Cthulhu cycle in "The Whisperer in Darkness."

Elsewhere, "Koth" is repeated in Grimlan's testament as "ye dedde citie of Koth, whereto no mortal man hath attained but mee," and in the final chant in the document, as "Ya—Koth!" (DG 256, 258). The same name appears in Lovecraft's novel, "The Case of Charles Dexter Ward," as "the sign of Koth, that dreamers see fixed above the archway of a certain black tower standing alone in twilight—and Willett did not like what his friend Randolph Carter had said of its powers" (H.P. Lovecraft,

"The Case of Charles Dexter Ward," in *At the Mountains of Madness and Other Novels*, texts selected by August Derleth, ed. S.T. Joshi, corrected seventh printing: Arkham House, 1991, p. 214). And in "The Dream-Quest of Unknown Kadath" as "the central tower with the sign of Koth" (*At the Mountains of Madness and Other Novels*, p. 342). Although written in 1927, "Charles Dexter Ward" did not see print until 1941. Similarly, "Unknown Kadath" was written in 1926–27 but not published until 1943.

To compound confusion about the origin and meaning of the term in Howard's fiction, "The Fire of Asshurbanipal" notes "the forgotten gods, Cthulhu and Koth and Yog-Sothoth," and in the Conan series and the science-fantasy novel *Almuric*, Howard uses "Koth" as a geographical and tribal name, respectively, with no evident Cthulhuvian associations.

The title of a celebrated Solomon Kane story is subtly namechecked among a litany of ominous phrases in Grimlan's testament: "There are skulls in ye stars" (DG 257). Conrad and Kirowan have the same names as characters in "The Children of the Night," and may or may not be the same individuals. Here, they react to scary situations in the nervous manner of Lovecraft's protagonists. As they approach Grimlan's house, Kirowan muses, "[T]he persistent swishing of a bat's wings somewhere overhead caused my taut nerves to jerk and thrum" (DG 247). This seems to be a foreshadowing of the supernatural chiropteran image at the end of the story, intentional or not. After the candles go out and Grimlan's body disappears, "[s]hrieking like damned men we broke down the door and fled frenziedly..." (DG 258).

The story's personification of supernatural forces is referred to in a mash-up of Biblical and Middle Eastern religious references: "the Prince of Darkness—Ahriman—the old Serpent—the veritable Satan!" (DG 252). And elsewhere, the "Black Master...men calle hym Sathanas & Beelzebub & Apolleon & Ahriman & Malik Tous..." (DG 257).

Most conspicuously, he is "Malik Tous...the title of the foul god worshipped by the mysterious Yezidees—they of Mount Alamout the Accursed—whose Eight Brazen Towers rise in the mysterious wastes of deep Asia" (DG 251). Another mash-up.

"Mount Alamout the Accursed" appears to be a variant on Alamut, the medieval fortress of the Shiite Ismaili sect, who were known to the Europeans as the Assassins. Alamut was located in what is now Iran, not central Asia, but its name and sinister reputation were appropriated by Robert W. Chambers as "Mount Alamout" for his 1920 novel *The Slayer of Souls*, from which Howard's usage seems to come. The "Yezidees" or Yezidis are a very real Kurdish group whose homeland was northern Iraq. Malik Tous or Tawsi Melek is their principal deity. Scholars of Howard's fiction have offered several possible sources for Howard's take on the Yezidees as a sinister cult and Malik Tous as a demonic figure, including the Robert W. Chambers novel and William Seabrook's colorful travel memoir, *Adventures in Arabia* (1927). Two substantial essays online, "The Brazen Peacock" by Karen Joan Khoutek and "The Satanic Robert E. Howard, Part 3" by Bobby Derie, provide further details and informed analyses. The threat of the "Yezidees" also lurks in a minor, Sax Rohmer-style adventure mystery by Howard, "The Brazen Peacock," published long after his death.

No longer as obscure an ethnic group as they were in Howard's day, the real Yezidis are frequently and tragically seen on CNN nowadays—persecuted, preyed upon, raped, and murdered by extremists and terrorists in today's ongoing violence in Iraq. It seems a safe bet that a Robert E. Howard writing in 2017 would portray them very differently than the Robert E. Howard of 1930–31 did, when gaudy fiction and sensationalistic non-fiction offered the only readily available sources of information or misinformation about these unfortunate people.

The Cthulhu references never quite line up coherently with the allusions to Malik Tous, except that here, as in "The Children of the Night," Howard seems to suggest that all obscure, malevolent cults are at some level related to each other, and that all of them, in some way, descend from the ancient veneration of the Old Ones. Grimlan refers to Malik Tous, the Dark Lord, as the lord of "ye Elder ones" (DG 256), indicating that in legend or fact a high position is held among the Old Ones by an entity that also appears across various religious systems as Satan, Ahriman, and other embodiments of ultimate evil. Readers who demand orderliness may be frustrated. Others may enjoy taking the sprawling details of the story and drawing their own imaginative conclusions.

"Untitled Fragment" ("Beneath the glare of the sun...")

First published in The Howard Collector, Spring 1967

Plot

Two archeologists, Brill and Allison, have excavated a mysterious dome in an unidentified Middle Eastern desert. From having delved into *Nameless Cults*, Brill suspects that it's the tomb of an ancient Stygian from the semi-mythic Hyborian Age. "It was the Stygians who built the pyramids and the Sphinx. And if I'm not mistaken, one of them lies in this pile of masonry" (UF 38). But Allison is skeptical.

Discussion

"Untitled Fragment" ends before the story proper really begins, but it intimates that the protagonists will unearth a relic or survival from the prehistoric Hyborian Age nation of Stygia. For Howard fans, it goes without saying that the Hyborian Age was the fictitious setting of the Conan stories, a fabulous era preceding the dawn of known history, in which Stygia with "its shadow-guarded tombs" figured prominently. (More about Conan and Cthulhu in Part IV of this informal guide.)

As far as I'm aware, we have no published information about the genesis of the "Untitled Fragment," or what Howard intended by suggesting an association with Conan's Hyborian Age. The association comes in Allison's remark about the "crazy German named Von Junzt" and his reference to *Nameless Cults* as the source of his knowledge about Stygia as a semi-mythic nation in "a sort of historical blind spot" that Von Junzt "called...the Hyborian Age" (UF 37). Consistent with details in Howard's fictitious historical summary, "The Hyborian Age," Allison (by way of Von Junzt) says that the ancient Egyptians descended from a prehistoric race produced by intermarriage of Stygia's native "lower classes" with an invading wave of "red-haired Nordics" before the end of the Hyborian Age.

My speculation is that the "Untitled Fragment" dates from 1933, and that Howard used (and in fact directly drew from) "The Hyborian Age" as a ready resource. Why 1933? In the summer of that year, Lovecraft told Howard by letter that one of his forthcoming stories "brings in Von Junzt and his Black Book as almost the central theme. It concerns a mummy found in the crypt of a Cyclopean stone temple of fabulous antiquity…" (H.P. Lovecraft, *Selected Letters IV, 1932–1934:* Arkham House, 1976, p. 222). The story was "Out of the Aeons," which Lovecraft prepared (adding the allusions to Von Junzt and other Mythos elements) from a manuscript by Hazel Heald. The story would appear two years later in *Weird Tales*, April 1935, as "Out of the Eons" under Heald's byline.

In the same letter, Lovecraft said, "Glad you enjoyed the *Witch House* and *Museum* story," a reference to two stories in the July 1933 *Weird Tales* that mentioned the German title devised by Lovecraft and Derleth, *Unaussprechlichen Kulten*, for the first time in print. "The Horror in the Museum," revised by Lovecraft from another Hazel Heald manuscript, adding Cthulhu references, appeared under Heald's byline. "The Dreams in the Witch-House" appeared under his own name.

I would suggest that the wheels began to spin in Howard's head, and he decided that it was a propitious time to resurrect Von Junzt in his own fiction, now that the eccentric German was ensconced in the Cthulhu mythology as part of two stories by the master, Lovecraft, with another yet to come. Acknowledging and using the German title *Unaussprechlichen Kulten* for the first and only time in his own fiction may have seemed like a further way to emphasize the internal consistency of the Mythos.

Unfortunately, 1933 was a shaky year professionally for Howard, as he faced the loss of some of his established markets and the impending loss of others, and scrambled to find footing in new genres. If I'm correct in my speculation that Howard began the story in 1933, then economic reality may have set in after a first rush of enthusiasm. He may have decided that his time would be better spent on something besides another Mythos story for *Weird Tales*. And so the story of Brill, Allison, and the Stygian tomb was left unfinished.

In any event, and not discounting any plausible theories that anyone else may want to suggest about its origins (or for that matter, any definitive evidence from Howard's papers that may come to light), "Untitled Fragment" offers a fascinating link between the Cthulhu and Conan mythologies through its reference to *Nameless Cults* as the source of Brill's knowledge about darkest Stygia. Another Howard horror fantasy set in modern times, "The Haunter of the Ring" (*Weird Tales*, June 1934), drew upon the Hyborian Age background. Its cast included characters named (John) Kirowan and O'Donnel(l), but it isn't clear whether these were supposed to be the Kirowan and O'Donnel who appear in "The Children of the Night," and the story doesn't include any direct Mythos references.

"Brill" and "Allison" are common character names in Howard's fiction, often applied to characters in fantasy, western, and boxing tales. Robert M. Price wrote a concluding segment for the "Untitled Fragment," and that finished version is published under the title "Black Eons" in Robert E. Howard et al., *Nameless Cults: The Cthulhu Mythos Fiction of Robert E. Howard*, edited by Robert M. Price (Chaosium Books, 2001).

"The Hoofed Thing"

First published in Weirdbook *No. 3, 1970, as "Usurp the Night"*

Plot

Searching for his fiancee Marjory Ash's missing cat in an unnamed small town or suburban neighborhood, Michael Strang encounters a newly arrived neighbor, John Stark. A powerfully muscled but apparently crippled scholar, Stark is well-versed in the sorts of esoteric studies that fascinate Strang. In his visit to Stark's rambling old house, Strang hears a noise upstairs, a scampering as of a small hoofed animal. On his next visit, the noise is louder. Over the next few weeks, more animals disappear, and an attempt is made to abduct Marjory's new pet, a bulldog, Bozo. Then children begin to vanish, then homeless people. The "stooped and shadowy figure" (HT 152) of a man is glimpsed by a couple making out in a secluded park. Strang begins to suspect John Stark, and when Marjory turns up missing, a bloodied Bozo leads Strang to the recluse's house. Stark has conjured an entity from "the blind dark Outer chasms" (HT 162) and penned it upstairs, feeding it a diet of animals and humans whom he has abducted. The creature has grown from the size of a toad to twice that of a man, and in the process it has become Stark's master. Strang bursts through the locked door to find Stark's dismembered body, and looming over it, the bloated, tentacled, hoofed, many-eyed form of the alien entity. Armed with a broadsword once wielded by a "Crusading ancestor" (HT 158), Strang hews the monster into pieces, and as he flees with Marjory and Bozo while the fragments of the creature melt into a "viscous black stenching fluid" (HT 168), he sets a fire that burns the house down and incinerates the creature.

Discussion

As did the creature in "The Thing on the Roof," the entity in "The Hoofed Thing" lumbers about on massive hoofs, only this time it doesn't lurk offstage, unseen by the narrator. It comes into plain view as a fully described "shape of nightmare and lunacy" (HT 166). A copy of *Nameless Cults*, the original German edition, clues Strang into the secret behind the noises in Stark's house and the occultist's "summoning of daemons out of the Void" (HT 156).

There are significant differences, in supporting details and overall mood, between this story and those of Howard's earlier Cthulhu tales that attempted to mimic Lovecraft's style. One striking discrepancy pertains to *Nameless Cults*: the question of its rarity.

In "The Black Stone," the original edition of Von Junzt's book is said to be so scarce that, the narrator estimates, "I doubt if there are more than half a dozen [copies] in the entire world today" (BN 153). In "The Thing on the Roof," it is "a task of no small magnitude" (TR 163-164), consuming three months of dedicated networking, for the narrator to locate a copy through his circle of scholars, specialists, and book dealers. Yet, in "The Hoofed Thing," Michael Strang happens to have this rare book in his personal library, and it comes into play by chance as he picks it off the shelf "at random" (HT 156) but fortuitously.

Ultimately defying the Lovecraft model of the bookish protagonist who runs away or faints when a Cthulhu entity materializes, Strang rushes to meet Stark's hoofed demon with mighty sword-strokes. Unlike the insular characters in the earlier stories where the Lovecraft style was strongest, Strang has a spirited girl friend who drives a roadster. His affection for the bulldog is obvious: "a waddling, bench-legged bulldog with a face like a gargoyle and as loyal a heart as ever beat in a canine breast" (HT 148)—perhaps a sibling from the same litter that produced Sailor Steve Costigan's bulldog Mike in Howard's boxing stories.

In contrast to the bookish scholars who inhabit gloomy, isolated manor houses in "The Children of the Night," "The Thing on the Roof," and "Dig Me No Grave," Strang and Marjory live in a quiet, everyday neighborhood with a make-out area in the local park. Stark's "rundown, rambling estate" (HT 145) is an anomaly in this setting rather than typical architecture. Strang's decision to face down the monster out of altruism, to forestall further horrors—"I owe it to the children—to the helpless people of this city" HT 165)—recalls the avenging spirit of Solomon Kane and the social consciousness of King Kull and King Conan in Howard's sword-and-sorcery stories.

Rusty Burke's indispensable timeline on the website Howard Works indicates that Howard unsuccessfully submitted the story in or around early 1932 to two markets. First, to *Strange Tales of Mystery and Terror*, a fantasy pulp in which "People of the Dark" appeared. Even though "The Hoofed Thing" failed to make the grade, it displays the characteristics of two other works that he did place with the magazine in 1932 and 1933: a faster pace, more action, and more character interplay than in his stories for *Weird Tales* that fervently mimicked Lovecraft's style. Lovecraft himself felt that the *Strange Tales* editors were "temperamentally opposed to material of the mood and style I produce" (Lovecraft, *Selected Letters IV, 1932–1934*, p. 7).

The second unsuccessful market for the story was a proposed magazine by an amateur publisher, Carl Swanson. Howard may have been alerted to Swanson by Lovecraft in the same January 16, 1932, letter quoted above. By May 7, 1932, Lovecraft reported that Swanson had "definitely abandoned" plans to launch a magazine (Lovecraft, *Selected Letters IV, 1932–1934*, p. 39), returning two stories that Lovecraft had sent to him, and presumably returning "The Hoofed Thing" to Howard.

As Robert M. Price has suggested, Lovecraft's "The Dunwich Horror" seems to have been Howard's inspiration for the concept of an extra-dimensional entity brought to earth and confined in a sealed room, where it grows and grows on a diet of flesh. The corresponding creature in the Lovecraft story is Wilbur Whateley's unseen brother, who "looked more like the father [Yog-Sothoth] than [Wilbur] did" (Lovecraft, *The Dunwich Horror and Others*, p. 198). A later Cthulhuvian story by August Derleth, "The Shuttered Room," first published in *The Shuttered Room & Other Pieces*, ed. August Derleth, Arkham House, 1959, features a similar concept of a creature shut away and growing in size in a locked room.

Another detail perhaps borrowed from Lovecraft, as Dr. Price has noted: a visitor to the Whateley house hears what "he thought…[was] a horse stamping on that floor above" (*The Dunwich Horror and Others*, p. 164). This image may have given Howard the idea for a hoofed creature in "The Thing on the Roof" and "The Hoofed Thing."

Howard's tale has been collected and anthologized some dozen times. This is a much less robust track record than that of his other Cthulhu stories. But then, the others had a four-decade headstart in first appearance.

Howard fans averse to the slow build-up and gothic atmosphere of the earlier stories may find the faster pace and sword-vs.-sorcery conclusion of "The Hoofed Thing" more to their taste. When Michael Strang goes after the monster with his ancestor's broadsword, and says that "demonic lust is no stronger than human hate, and…I will match this blade, which in old days slew witches and warlocks and vampires and werewolves, against the foul legions of Hell itself" (HT 165), we wonder if he has been temporarily possessed by Solomon Kane or Conan.

"[D]rawn from the shapeless void and materialized into concrete substance, the fiend was vulnerable to material weapons," Strang muses (HT 167). Similarly, in "The Vale of Lost Women," Conan boasts that "when [demonic entities come to earth], they have to take on earthly form and flesh of some sort. A man like myself, with a sword, is a match for any amount of fangs and talons, infernal or terrestrial" ("The Vale of Lost Women," in Robert E. Howard, *The Coming of Conan the Cimmerian*, Ballantine Books/Del Rey, 2003, p. 316). Strang's sword has divine attributes—"a saint had blessed [it] in old times against the powers of darkness" (HT 167)—but it's unclear whether this fact makes the weapon any more potent than it already is as heavy edged steel.

As in some other Howard stories, the two central male characters of "The Hoofed Thing" are alike physically and temperamentally, but ultimately they stand in opposition to each other on different sides of the line between good and evil. Strang's "powerful frame" is mirrored in Stark's "thick short neck and massive shoulders" (HT 167, 146). Both men are versed in obscure scholarly matters, such as the "anthropological researches of Professor Hendryk Brooler" (HT 147). Although Stark doesn't specifically say that his study of "blasphemous books" included perusal of the *Necronomicon*, we may assume that he, like Strang, is familiar with Alhazred's tome. A bit of Lovecraft creeps into the portrait of Strang when he first sees Stark's monster, and "[averts his] eyes from that grisly head for the sake of [his] sanity." But shortly he finds his Howard mojo and attacks the creature in "a red blaze of berserker fury" (HT 167).

For today's readers, the quiet neighborhood setting of the story, the well-adjusted protagonist and his comely fiancée in peril, the shadowy figure glimpsed from lovers' lane, the faithful canine pet, and the full-on appearance of the monster at the end anticipate the stock elements of the science fiction-horror movies of the 1950s. It's pleasant to imagine an alternate universe in which Howard lived into the Space Age, became a screenwriter for Universal-International Pictures, and worked with directors Jack Arnold and Nathan Juran one month on Audie Murphy westerns and the next on Arthur

Franz monster movies. Come to think of it, why not a film with modern CGI as a vehicle for Vin Diesel or Dwayne Johnson as Howard's suburban sword-wielding hero?

"Black John's Vengeance"
First published in From Beyond the Dark Gateway No. 3, April 1974, *as "The Black Bear Bites"*

Plot
Bill Lannon, a former British agent, is murdered while investigating sinister conclaves at the house of the wealthy, crooked Chinese merchant Yotai Yun outside Hankow. Black John O'Donnell vows to avenge his friend and sneaks into Yotai's heavily guarded house. There, he sees Yotai and a diverse group of Asian criminals and outwardly respectable pillars of Chinese society meeting with a masked figure, the semi-mythic Hooded Lama. The Lama pledges to lead a revolt against Westerners in China under the banner of the Old Ones. Once Yotai and the Lama are alone and overheard by Black John, they reveal that the Lama is an impostor who only pretends to be a priest of the Old Ones in order to incite an uprising. Discovered, O'Donnell shoots it out with the two conspirators, killing them but taking bullets himself. The police arrive before Yotai's servants can finish the job. Black John unmasks the hooded Lama and discovers that it is one of his other acquaintances, English club-goer Eric Brand.

Discussion
"Black John's Vengeance," also known as "The Black Bear Bites," was sent to *Argosy* in April 1931, and later rejected, following earlier rejection by *Adventure* and *Far East* magazines. The tale suggests the influence of Sax Rohmer's stories about Asian conspiracies against the West, such as "The Black Mandarin" (1922) and the Fu Manchu series. For pulp editors, the derivative theme and the references to the then-obscure Lovecraft mythology may have derailed the story as an adventure yarn.

One wonders whether it would have scored with *Weird Tales* had Howard strengthened the Cthulhu Mythos aspect and added some forthright fantasy elements. It could have been re-imagined and revised, perhaps, as a sequel to the highly successful "Skull-Face," with the Hooded Lama as an actual votary of Cthulhu—with all that that association implies in terms of occult powers at his disposal—who steps in to reassemble Kathulos' criminal network following the Atlantean's presumed death.

The allusions to the Cthulhu cycle come when the Hooded Lama masquerades as the priest of "an old and evil religion," a "terrible cult, which had slumbered for so many thousands of years in the wastes of Mongolia" (BV 135–136). Led by "the prophet of the Old Ones," the disaffected of Asia could anticipate that "the great Cthulhu would sweep them all to victory" (BV 136). Later, asked if he fears retribution by "the real priests of Yog-Sototh" for his imposture, the Hooded Lama says, "I do not fear the Mongolian devil-worshippers" (BV 139).

Howard seems to be extrapolating from a passage in "The Call of Cthulhu," in which we learn that the underground worship of Cthulhu survives in part through "the undying leaders of the cult in the mountains of China" (Lovecraft, *The Call of Cthulhu and Other Weird Stories*, p. 154). The reference to Mongolia also calls to mind a passage in "Dig Me No Grave," in which Conrad recalls that John Grimlan gave him sealed instructions for the disposition of his body following his death, "immediately after his return from Mongolia" (DG 250), presumably where Grimlan had his final meeting with the Black Master to whom he had bartered his soul.

The Hooded Lama declares that the great Asian conquerors had deferred to the "evilly old" cult of Cthulhu: "Genghis Khan had bowed before its priests, and Tamerlane, and centuries before them, Attila" (BV 135). Today, when mash-ups of historical swashbuckling and fantasy are becoming more common, as in the movie *The Great Wall* (2017), a present-day Howard might have been intrigued by the possibility of introducing the Mythos into Genghis Khan's world of *Red Blades of Black Cathay* (1931) or the court of Tamerlane in *Lord of Samarcand* (1932).

Black John is the prototypical straight-talking, iron-fisted Howard character: "a rough sailorman, uncultured and untaught in sophist ways" (BV 134). This is very close to the verse at the head of Chapter V of the Conan story, "The

Phoenix on the Sword," presumably embodying the philosophy of Conan himself: "What do I know of cultured ways, the gilt, the craft and the lie. ... The subtle tongue, the sophist guile, they fail when the broadswords sing..." (*The Coming of Conan the Cimmerian*, p. 19).

Does a story about fraud perpetrated in the names of Cthulhu, Yog-Sothoth, and the Old Ones qualify as a Cthulhu story? It's debatable, but Howard provides an apparent linkage with a bit of authentic Cthulhu lore from Lovecraft himself. And even if the Hooded Lama is a fake, there's no indication that the characters in the story regard the shadowy Mongolian cult of the Old Ones, itself, as a pretense. So in it goes.

"Dagon Manor"
First published in The "New" Howard Reader No. 3, *November 1998*

Plot
The unnamed narrator and his friend Conrad approach "Dagon Manor, the accursed" (DM 24), the home of their acquaintance Tavarel. When they knock on the door, they are greeted by Tavarel's manservant Ketric, whose "bare, high skull...cold light eyes, and...thin hooded nose" remind the narrator repugnantly of "a vulture or some foul bird of prey" (DM 24).

Discussion
The names "Conrad" and "Tavarel" suggest that these are the same characters who appeared in "The Children of the Night," although there the latter name was spelled "Taverel." The names "Tavarel," "Taverel," "Tavrel," and "Taferal" appear in several Howard stories; "Taverel Manor" was the title of the unfinished (and in the preliminary form in which Howard left it, uninspired) sequel to "Skull-Face." Howard used the pseudonym "John Taverel" for two tales submitted to *Ghost Stories* magazine.

Whether this seven-paragraph fragment would have been another story featuring the Conrad, Kirowan, and Taverel of "The Children of the Night," whether Howard actually retooled it as "The Children of the Night" as some have suggested, given the similarity of names in "Ketric" and "Ketrick," or whether it would have been linked with the Cthulhu Mythos—all of these questions leave room for speculation. I assume that an association with the Cthulhu cycle was intended, given the inclusion of "Dagon" in the title and the appearance of characters who at least have the same names as those who also featured in "The Children of the Night."

Howard seems to have salvaged the bleak description of the setting—"the lonely desolation of the fens" (DM 24)—in imagining the gothic geography of "Worms of the Earth." The late C.J. Henderson expanded and completed the fragment for publication in *Shudder Stories* #4, March 1986. Publication in *The "New" Howard Reader* represented the first appearance of the pure-text Howard fragment.

"The House" (unfinished story)
First published in The Howard Reader *#8, August 2003*

Plot
Conrad and Kirowan puzzle over a mysterious turning point in the life of the poet Justin Geoffrey, "half genius, half maniac" (TH 19). By all accounts, Geoffrey lived a mundane existence in a stolid middle-class family until age ten, when he began to be tormented by nightmares that he shaped into horrific, outré verse. Conrad believes that the change in the boy occurred after he spent a night sleeping inside a circle of oak trees around a deserted old house outside Old Dutchtown, near the New York Catskills. Skuyler, a friend of Conrad's and an artist specializing in weird subject matter, had painted a canvas of the house, which he says "exudes an aura of abnormality" (TH 21). The three men travel to Old Dutchtown to gather more information and view the house. The mayor says the title to the property is disputed by two farmers, each of whom asserts that the land is owned by the other one, and that no one has been able to enter the barred and bolted house. Conrad, Kirowan, and Skuyler continue to investigate, passing through the circle of trees to approach the house. There the unfinished Howard fragment ends.

Discussion

Another story featuring friends named Kirowan and Conrad, except the Conrad in this story is named "James" rather than "John," the first name of the character in "Dig Me No Grave." Same Conrad? Same Kirowan?

The upstate New York locale, with its Dutch cultural influence and "atmosphere of decadence," may reflect the Catskills setting in Lovecraft's "The Lurking Fear" (*Weird Tales*, June 1928), with its "antique, grove-circled" Martense mansion of sinister reputation (H.P. Lovecraft, "The Lurking Fear," *Dagon and Other Macabre Tales*, Arkham House, corrected seventh printing, 1991, p. 180). Or it may have carried over from correspondence in 1931 with Wilfred Blanch Talman of New York, a friend of Lovecraft's. Or both. In the correspondence with Talman, Howard expressed interest in the Dutch phase of colonial New York history after Talman commented on some points of Dutch influence in New York (*SL 1931–1936*, pp. 12–14).

Where "The Black Stone" and "The Thing on the Roof" provided data-dumps on Von Junzt and *Nameless Cults*, "The House" offers similar filling-in of information for Howard's other major contribution to the Cthulhu cycle, the mad poet Justin Geoffrey. One wonders whether it was intended as the third entry in a trilogy initiated by the earlier stories, since it is so closely linked with them, and why Howard failed to complete it. Perhaps at that point, he had wearied of imitating the claustrophobic Lovecraft style.

Adding to the imaginary bibliography of Geoffrey's work, "The House" includes two new, short verses attributed to him, one beginning "Behind the Veil, what gulfs...", and the other, "Drowsy and dull with age..." (TH 19–20, 21). The first-named, four-line verse saw independent publication by Howard in the September 1932 *Weird Tales* as "An Open Window." Howard included the second-named, four-line poem in a December 1931 letter to Lovecraft. He also published it under the title "Arkham" in the August 1932 issue of *Weird Tales*. (More about the short and tragic life of Justin Geoffrey in Part V, "Howard's Defining Additions to Cthulhu Lore.")

In addition to rounding out the biographical sketch of Justin Geoffrey begun in the earlier stories, "The House" also provides surprisingly frank and poignant glimpses into Howard's own temperament and habits.

In a September 1931 letter to Wilfred Blanch Talman, Howard remarked that he "always hated school" (*SL 1931–1936*, p. 12). Similarly, Conrad states that Geoffrey "despised and detested the courses of education given in school" (TH 20). Conrad elaborates, saying that Geoffrey "condemned the triviality and uselessness" of formal education (TH 20). "Things I have discovered to be of most use, I learned mostly without formal education," Howard told Lovecraft in a 1933 letter (*SL 1931–1936*, p. 54). Geoffrey was a "tireless searcher for knowledge, but it was knowledge of his own choosing" (TH 20).

Conrad comments that Geoffrey was "stubbornly perverse in his use of obsolete words and archaic phrases" (TH 20). This observation recalls E. Hoffman Price's remark that Howard "pronounced the 'w' in 'sword' very clearly; and 'wound'—that which Conan inflicted so prodigiously and lavishly—was invariably pronounced to rhyme with 'sound.'" Howard's parents "had no such eccentricities of speech," Price observed, concluding it was "very possible that Robert deliberately affected an Elizabethan pronunciation" (E. Hoffman Price, "A Memory of R.E. Howard," in *The Last Celt: A Bio-Bibliography of Robert Ervin Howard*, edited and compiled by Glenn Lord: Donald M. Grant, Publisher, 1976, p. 82).

Conrad remarks upon Geoffrey's intellectual isolation from his "intolerably dull family," who believed that "any one who [did] not make his living by selling potatoes [was] abnormal" (TH 20). Howard's parents were more indulgent, but the passage recalls E. Hoffman Price's poignant rumination on Howard as at least a self-perceived outsider in his home town of Cross Plains, Texas: "A writer, I gathered, [was] regarded as a harmless freak. ... Robert must always have felt himself to be, whether he wanted to or not, someone and something apart from the standard model Texan" (Price, "A Memory of R.E. Howard," p. 84).

Decades after Howard's death, August Derleth ably concluded the unfinished fragment of "The House" under the title "The House in the Oaks." It appeared shortly after Derleth's own death in his anthology of original horror tales for

Arkham House, *Dark Things* (1971). It's impossible to say how Howard would have developed the story, but Derleth plausibly and effectively follows on from a suggestion in Geoffrey's/Howard's verse, "Behind the Veil, what gulfs..." This version was collected in an omnibus edition of Derleth's Cthulhu stories, *In Lovecraft's Shadow* (Mycroft & Moran, 1998). The pure-text Howard fragment without Derleth's contribution was unpublished until 2003.

Lovecraft adopted Justin Geoffrey into his own Cthulhu fiction, securing Howard's creation as part of the sprawling Mythos just as he had previously incorporated Von Junzt and *Nameless Cults*. In "The Thing on the Doorstep" (*Weird Tales*, January 1937), Lovecraft's character Edward Pickman Derby "was a close correspondent of the notorious Baudelairean poet Justin Geoffrey, who wrote *The People of the Monolith* and died screaming in a madhouse in 1926 after a visit to a sinister, ill-regarded village in Hungary" (*The Dunwich Horror and Others*, p. 277).

Geoffrey also figures by reference in some later Cthulhu stories. In Brian Lumley's "The Second Wish," a modern visitor to Hungary finds Justin Geoffrey's signature, along with that of Lovecraft's Charles Dexter Ward, in an old hotel ledger (Brian Lumley, "The Second Wish," in *New Tales of the Cthulhu Mythos*, ed. Ramsey Campbell: Arkham House, 1980, p. 83). In Lin Carter's "The Winfield Heritance," *The People of the Monolith* is paired with Edward Pickman Derby's *Azathoth and Other Horrors* in Hiram Winfield's library (Lin Carter, "The Winfield Heritance," in *The Xothic Legend: The Complete Mythos Fiction of Lin Carter*, ed. Robert M. Price: Chaosium, 1997).

PART III
Howard's Lovecraft-Influenced Work Outside the Mythos

I've identified four works as associated stories that reflect Lovecraft's thematic or stylistic influence, even if they are not Cthulhu stories, strictly speaking. The amorphous creature in "The Footfalls Within," which is a later story in Howard's Solomon Kane series, and the cosmically horrific entity in "The Cairn on the Headland" are Cthulhuvian in all but name. "The Dwellers Under the Tomb" is not a Cthulhu story but nonetheless derives its central feature from another product of Lovecraft's imagination. "The Noseless Horror" so blatantly and effectively opens as a pastiche of Lovecraft's style that I would feel remiss in not noting it.

"The Footfalls Within"
First published in Weird Tales, *September 1931*
Plot
The sixteenth century Puritan adventurer Solomon Kane is captured by slavers in the African jungle. On their trek back to market, the slavers come across a large, ancient structure like a mausoleum. Yussef, one of the party, an elderly man of learning, advises that they leave the vault alone. Kane senses the sound or vibration of heavy footsteps from within the mausoleum. Hassim, the head slaver, decides to break into the structure, expecting to find riches inside. Instead, he unintentionally releases an amorphous, rampaging entity,

which kills Hassim as the others flee. Although the thing is impervious to steel, Kane is able to slay it with his mystic, cat-headed staff, which he had been given by a witch doctor in an earlier adventure.

Discussion

Solomon Kane was one of Howard's earliest published series characters, and five of the stories in the series had already appeared in *Weird Tales* when "The Footfalls Within" was published. The tale demonstrates a profound Lovecraft influence, unlike the more traditional ghostly and vampiric horrors of previous stories in the series written before 1930, as Kane ponders on the nature of the entity from the mausoleum as an organism from long eons ago: "The planet men call the earth spun on through the untold ages…and as it spun it spawned Life, and living things which wriggled about it as maggots are spawned in rot and corruption. Man was the dominant maggot now—why should he in his pride suppose that he and his adjuncts were the first maggots—or the last to rule a planet quick with unguessed life?" (FW 344).

Like the Mythos entities, the creature is characterized by a "nauseous burst of unholy stench" (FW 343). Its "tramp of monstrous feet from within that ghastly mausoleum" (FW 341) evokes the heavy footsteps of the monsters in "The Thing on the Roof" and "The Hoofed Thing." Only the lack of an explicit reference to Cthulhu, Yog-Sothoth, or the *Necronomicon* disqualifies it from being classified as a Mythos story. Even so, a reference to "strange, dark pre-Adamite priests in the silent cities beneath the seas" (FW 335) comes pretty close, and the Lovecraftian rhetoric flows freely, for example: "Kane's fright was like a cold wind blowing on him from outer realms of unguessed Darkness" (FW 342) and "somewhere down the dim vistas of his soul's consciousness re-echoed unbearably a hideous formless cataclysm" (FW 343).

One wonders whether the published version of the story was preceded by a draft that included allusions to the Cthulhu entities by name?

"The Cairn on the Headland"

First published in Strange Tales of Mystery and Terror, *January 1933*

Plot

American scholar James O'Brien and his unwelcome companion and blackmailer Ortali travel to Dublin to investigate a mysterious pile of stones, Grimmin's Cairn. Ortali determines to break into the cairn to get at valuables he believes are buried there, and coerces O'Brien into agreeing to help him do so that night. O'Brien encounters an elderly Irishwoman in outmoded dress, also an O'Brien by birth, who gives him an ancient cross and says an "ancient evil" stirs. That night, O'Brien falls asleep with a stone from the cairn in his pocket, and relives the aftermath of the Battle of Clontarf between the Irish and the Norse in 1014, when as an Irish warrior, Red Cumal, he helped to inter Odin, the Norse god, slain in the battle by a spear with a cross carved in the blade. He realizes that Odin is the "Gray Man" buried in Grimmin's Cairn, and rushing there, he witnesses the pagan god rise and begin to transform when a spring of holly falling on Odin's chest releases him from the "fleshly prison" of his earthly body. Altering into his true, towering demonic form, he slays Ortali. With his ancient cross, the gift of his elderly kinswoman—actually long dead but returned briefly from the grave to arm him against the resurrected Odin—O'Brien banishes the demon back to "the dark limbo which gave him birth."

Discussion

Apparently retrieving and reworking historical material about the Irish vs. the Danes that he had used without commercial success in writing two previous stories about the Battle of Clontarf—one a straight historical adventure ("Spears of Clontarf") and the other a sword-and-sorcery historical fantasy rewritten from the first one ("The Gray God Passes")—Howard ingeniously merged his interest in Irish history with Cthulhuvian-style fantasy in "The Cairn on the Headland."

In "The Grey God Passes," alternatively titled "The Twilight of the Grey Gods" in at least one reprinting, Odin takes anthropomorphic form as "a tall man, wrapped in a cloak beneath which...[was] a sheen of mail. The stranger wore a slouch hat pulled so low that from his shadowed features only one eye gleamed, cold and grim as the grey sea" (Robert E. Howard, "The Grey God Passes," in *Swords of the North*: REH Foundation Press, 2014, p. 247). Later he grows "monstrously in stature...[and] loomed colossal among the clouds...suddenly grey, as with vast age" (p. 249). In a final glimpse after the Norse defeat, he is "a vague, gigantic form" in the storm clouds, "beard and wild locks streaming in the gale, cloak billowing out like great wings" (p. 279). He "returns to the blue gulfs of the North which gave him birth" (p. 280).

"Spears of Clontarf" was submitted unsuccessfully to both *Adventure* and *Argosy* in summer 1931, and "The Grey God Passes" was rejected by *Weird Tales* later in the year. In a fast turnaround and publication, "The Cairn on the Headland" scored a sale with *Strange Tales* around January 1933. Its modern-day setting—with the heroic fantasy content relegated to the equivalent of a flashback, as in "People of the Dark"—better conformed to the style that *Strange Tales* seemed to prefer (a primarily modern setting and character interplay) than the all-out medieval carnage of "The Grey God Passes" would have.

The phantasmagorical depiction of Odin in "The Grey God Passes" is imaginatively impressive, his "gigantic form" in the sky reminiscent of August Derleth's Cthulhu entity Ithaqua in "The Thing That Walked on the Wind," which coincidentally ran in the same issue of *Strange Tales* as "The Cairn on the Headland." But Howard's decision to go the next step, and picture the Norse god instead as an unearthly entity that ultimately sheds its human shape, is inspired: "[T]he fiendish spirit of ice and frost and darkness that the sons of the North deified as Odin, stood nakedly and terribly in the stars. About his grisly head played lightnings and the shuddering gleams of the aurora. His towering anthropomorphic form was dark as shadow and gleaming as ice; his horrible crest reared colossally against the vaulting arch of the sky" (CH 211–212).

Much like his incorporation of Lovecraftian cosmic horror in the Conan stories, this is a clever mash-up that merges a measure of heroic fantasy with an element suggestive of the Cthulhu entities without actually crossing over into the Mythos proper.

O'Brien's use of a cross to banish the demon may remind the reader of the "quotation" from the *Necronomicon* at the beginning of Frank Belknap Long's "The Space-Eaters": "The cross is not a passive agent. It protects the pure of heart, and it has often appeared in the air above our sabbats, confusing and dispersing the powers of Darkness" (Frank Belknap Long, "The Space-Eaters," in *The Hounds of Tindalos*: Arkham House, 1946, p. 166). Howard doesn't appear to have been particularly religious in the dogmatic sense, so his use of a cross seems to be more of a horror-story convention than any personal statement of Christian doctrine such as, for example, the Catholicism of William Peter Blatty's *The Exorcist* (1971).

When O'Brien regards the Cross of Saint Brandon "reverently" (CH 200), the value of the relic seems to rest more in its "archaic and unmistakably Celtic" origin (CH 199) than in its religious symbolism. The intervention of O'Brien's long-deceased kinswoman recalls other Howard tales in which the ghost of a relative, sweetheart, friend, or mentor saves the protagonist from death. In "Dermod's Bane," unpublished during Howard's lifetime, ancient evil persists in modern-day Ireland, as it does in "The Cairn on the Headland," and the ghost of the Irish-American narrator's deceased sister saves him from the malicious spirit of a medieval Irish outlaw.

"The Noseless Horror"
First published in Magazine of Horror
No. 31, February 1970

Plot
The narrator, named Slade, and his friend John Gordon accept an invitation to visit the Egyptologist Sir Thomas Cameron at his remote English estate. They do so even though they personally dislike the ruthless Cameron. Among other questionable actions, Cameron intentionally misled a rival, Gustav Von Honmann, into searching for a fabled city in a dangerous area of Central Africa where he was killed by a hostile tribe.

Cameron now wishes to validate an unusual discovery, the finding of a strange mummy in upper Egypt. That night, Cameron is fatally stabbed; dying in manic hysteria, he gasps, "the noseless one" (NH 101). Suspicion falls on his manservant, a Sikh, Ganra Singh, whose nose had been slashed off in a battle when he served in the Anglo-Indian army. It transpires that the murderer was the now-reanimated mummy. When the creature attacks Slade and Gordon, Ganra rushes in and hurls it into the fireplace. Before the mummy burns up, the heat momentarily inflates its shrunken features, and Slade recognizes the face of the vengeful Von Honmann.

Discussion

"The Noseless Horror," unpublished until long after Howard's death, opens ominously: "Abysses of unknown terror lie veiled by the mists which separate man's everyday life from the uncharted and unguessed realms of the supernatural. ... The rending of the veil between the worlds of reality and of the occult is often a hideous experience" (NH 95). This seems to be Howard's paraphrase of Lovecraft's famous opening from "The Call of Cthulhu": "We live on a placid island of ignorance in the midst of black seas of infinity...the piecing together of dissociated knowledge will open up...terrifying vistas of reality" (*The Call of Cthulhu and Other Weird Stories*, p. 139).

The protagonist, Slade, exhibits the usual reaction of a Lovecraft protagonist as he senses something horrible lurking nearby: "[I]n that silent darkened corridor...I came as near to insanity as I have ever come..." (NH 105). However, he and Gordon man up in true Howard style when the time comes to defend themselves against the supernatural menace.

Although Howard's opening bears the clear stamp of Lovecraft, he stops short of invoking the Cthulhu cycle. The story of a reanimated mummy relies on an "occult" premise, so defined by Gordon: "[T]o bridge the gulf which lies between the two worlds of life and death, the spirit or ghost must inhabit and animate a fleshly form—preferably its own former habitation" (NH 109). Lovecraft suggests that true "reality" encompasses not only our material world but also realms beyond our knowledge and senses. Howard implies that reality is limited to the material world, and anything else is part of the supernatural or occult.

Along with the flavor of Lovecraft, "The Noseless Horror" also strongly suggests the influence of Sax Rohmer's exotic thrillers, although it hinges on a supernatural element and Rohmer rarely used occult themes in his stories. The disfigured, initially suspect, but courageous Ganra Singh is reminiscent of the stalwart Sikh Indian soldiers with whom Howard would have been familiar as characters in Talbot Mundy's stories that he read in *Adventure* magazine.

It's possible but questionable whether the iconic Boris Karloff movie *The Mummy* was another influence. *The Mummy* didn't open until the end of 1932. In style and trappings, "The Noseless Horror" seems to belong to the earlier period of 1928–30, when Howard wrote and published the similarly Rohmer-influenced "Skull-Face" and first began emulating Lovecraft. However, Howard was still marketing some Lovecraftian fiction in 1932 (such as "The Dwellers Under the Tomb," noted below, which *Weird Tales* rejected in May 1932), so a later date of composition isn't impossible.

The John Gordon of this story, "a wealthy sportsman" (NH 95), appears not to be the British intelligence agent of the same name who is featured in "Skull-Face," but both men display a similar brusqueness and nervous energy in their personalities. With a little more care and elaboration, "The Noseless Horror," like "Black John's Vengeance," could have been rethought and rebooted into different form as a worthy sequel to "Skull-Face." Certainly, it would have been a more promising sequel than the one suggested by the existing and anemic opening paragraphs of "Taverel Manor," the actual unfinished sequel.

"The Dwellers Under the Tomb"
First published in Lost Fantasies No. 4, *1976*

Plot
Conrad and his guest O'Donnel are awakened late at night by Job Kiles, an elderly miser who lives nearby. Hysterically, he swears that his brother Jonas, who died the night before,

returned that night and peered through his window. He fears that Jonas has come back as a vampire. Conrad and O'Donnel agree to accompany Job to the family tomb in the Dagoth Hills, to make sure that Jonas' body still rests in his casket. Hearing what seems to be his dead brother's voice and preceding the other two men into the tomb, Job rushes out, babbling "the thing in the coffin!" and falls dead of apparent shock. Jacob's coffin is empty. In a tunnel beyond the tomb, the two adventurers find Jacob's diary, which reveals that Jacob planned to feign death, and to trick Job into believing that he had returned as a vampire. Knowing that Job superstitiously would come to the tomb to drive a stake into his heart, he planned to kill Job and assume his identity and his fortune. In the deep tunnels, Conrad and O'Donnel encounter monsters: vile-smelling ghouls with canine features. O'Donnel shoots their way out, and they find Jacob's mangled body inside another door to the outside, where he had been killed by the ghouls on returning from Job's house. Before the door slams behind them as they rush outside, they have a final horrific glimpse of the body, and over it crouching one of the dwellers under the tomb.

Discussion

Another Conrad and O'Donnel, who may be the same individuals from "The Children of the Night," or different people entirely. Howard's growing inclination to incorporate his Southwestern heritage into his fiction is reflected in Conrad's remark as O'Donnel straps on a .45 pistol: "Can't forget your Texas raising, can you?" (DU 320). The opening of the tale recalls the first paragraphs of other gothic horror stories by Howard, with its portrait of a "dark house looming gaunt and silent" in a dreary landscape (DU 321).

This time, in an apparent tip of the hat to Lovecraft, the story is set in New England rather than Great Britain. O'Donnel notes that the name "Dagoth Hills," although "not allied to any known Indian language, yet [was] used first by the red men to designate this stunted range" (DU 321). The similarity to Lovecraft's "Dagon" and "Yog-Sothoth" is obvious. In the Conan story "The Scarlet Citadel," the name is used in a different but similarly sinister context, "men say that a dancing-girl of Shadizar slept too near the pre-human ruins on Dagoth Hill and woke in the grip of a black demon..." (*The Coming of Conan the Cimmerian*, p. 103).

The primary Lovecraft influence in "The Dwellers Under the Tomb" isn't the Cthulhu mythology but rather Lovecraft's story "Pickman's Model." Howard's ghoulish dwellers are "gray, shambling monstrosit[ies]," "flaming-eyed dog-headed horror[s] such as madmen see in black nightmares" (DU 334). Compare Lovecraft's description of his tunnel-dwelling, grave-robbing ghouls: "the dog face with its pointed ears, bloodshot eyes, flat nose, and drooling lips" (*The Dunwich Horror and Others*, p. 23). Howard's place name of Pirate Hill recalls Lovecraft's Gallows Hill. Conrad and O'Donnel react to their encounter with the hysteria of typical Lovecraft characters: "In a frenzy we leaped at the door—tore at the key—hurled open the door" (DU 336).

As Lovecraft says that "the dog-things" in his story "were developed from mortals" (*The Dunwich Horror and Others*, p. 19), Howard suggests that the dwellers under the tomb were descended from a forgotten human race that "resembled the Caucasoid type rather than the Indian" (DU 333). As in his stories about the Children of the Night, Howard is fascinated by the prospect that isolated societies of humans will degenerate, mutate, and retreat underground under certain circumstances, becoming something less than human in the process—"the nadir of human degeneration" (DU 336).

PART IV
Cthulhu and Conan

When he began to write about Conan the Cimmerian in the spring of 1932 (see Patrice Louinet's "Hyborian Genesis: Notes on the Creation of the Conan Stories," in *The Coming of Conan the Cimmerian*: Ballantine Books/Del Rey, 2003), it seems that Howard contemplated a crossover between the Cthulhu cycle and the matter of the Hyborian Age. Louinet reports that the first, unsubmitted draft of the inaugural Conan adventure, "The Phoenix on the Sword," contained references to "Cthulhu, Tsathogua, Yog-Sothoth, and the Nameless Old Ones." Howard then rewrote the story and trimmed all references but "the Nameless Old Ones." This rewritten version was the one that Howard sent to *Weird Tales* (*The Coming of Conan the Cimmerian*, p. 436).

Perhaps Howard initially believed that explicit references to the Cthulhu mythology would help establish the Conan series with *Weird Tales* readers. Ultimately, by striking all but one of the names from the version that he sent to editor Farnsworth Wright, he may have concluded that the new series should stand on its own, and that tying it in too closely with Cthulhu might be more of a liability than an asset in the long run.

Aside from a halting effort begun but put aside—the "Untitled Fragment" ("Beneath the glare of the sun...") discussed earlier in this informal guide—Howard never again tried to combine the mythology of Conan's Hyborian Age with the formal mythology of the Cthulhu Mythos. Nevertheless, the Conan series displays the influence of Lovecraft and Cthulhu in its underlying concept of sorcery, or at least one type of sorcery, as a process for summoning creatures from outer space or other dimensions through the use of infernal spells. In the same manner, modern-day characters in Lovecraft's and Howard's Mythos stories summon similar entities by using obscure formulae gleaned from the *Necronomicon* and *Nameless Cults*.

As Charles Hoffman and Marc Cerasini have noted, "Cthulhoid abominations comprise a significant percentage of the evil forces that heroes like Conan strive against" (Hoffman and Cersaini, "The Strange Case of Robert Ervin Howard," in *The Horror of It All*, edited by Robert M. Price, The Borgo Press, 1990, p. 97). Examples of these loathsome horrors are:

- The nameless demon summoned by the sorcerer Thoth-Amon in "The Phoenix on the Sword": "a great black thing...born in no sane or human world. ... [T]he Cimmerian glimpsed the reality of all the abysmal and blasphemous horrors that lurk in the outer darkness of formless voids and nighted gulfs" (*The Coming of Conan the Cimmerian*, pp. 25, 25). Likened in one sentence to "a great black hound" (p. 24), the creature is also reminiscent of the infernal title horror in Lovecraft's story "The Hound" (*Weird Tales*, September 1929).

- Thaug in "A Witch Shall Be Born": "a vast dark form... rushing...in gigantic frog-like leaps ... a black shapelessness in which only the staring eyes and gleaming fangs were distinct" (*The Coming of Conan the Cimmerian*, pp. 297, 298).

- Thog in "Xuthal of the Dusk": "a black nightmare shape that could only have been bred in the lost pits of hell" (*The Coming of Conan the Cimmerian*, p. 241). Howard's disturbing rape imagery as the monster fondles Conan's naked girlfriend Natala foreshadows the salacious special effects in the present-day genre of Japanese monster-horror-porn movies: "A dark tentacle-like member slid about her body, and she screamed at the touch of it on her naked flesh. ... All the obscenity and salacious infamy spawned in the muck of the abysmal pits of Life seemed to drown her in seas of cosmic filth" (p. 238).

A note about Thog, who regards the nude Natala with "cosmic lust" (p. 238) and embraces her in a "lustful grasp" (p.

241): The late Fritz Leiber described the creature as "an amorphous and ravening Lovecraftian monster with the addition of an unlikely sexual hunger" (Fritz Leiber, "Review of *Conan the Adventurer,*" in *The Howard Collector* No. 10, Spring 1968, p. 40). It seems that Mr. Leiber was thinking of Lovecraft's admonition that "non-human beings would be wholly apart from human motives and perspectives" (H.P. Lovecraft, "Some Notes on Interplanetary Fiction," in *Miscellaneous Writings*, ed. S.T. Joshi, Arkham House, 1995, p. 121).

One such motive unlikely in an alien lifeform surely would be an impulse toward sexual violence against women. And yet Lovecraft thought highly of the "cumulative suspense and ultimate horror" of Arthur Machen's story "The Great God Pan," in which an extra-dimensional entity identified with the mythic god Pan impregnates a young woman, seemingly through rape (H.P. Lovecraft, "Supernatural Horror in Literature," in *Dagon and Other Macabre Tales*, Arkham House, corrected seventh printing, 1991, p. 423). Even Lovecraft, or especially Lovecraft, must have recognized the transgressive power of imagery linking the supernatural, violence, and sexual intercourse.

Actually, Lovecraft himself dealt with supernatural hybridization in "The Dunwich Horror," which seems to have been inspired by the Machen story, as observers such as Robert M. Price have noted. In "The Dunwich Horror," a grotesque bumpkin named Wilbur Whateley is the offspring of a strange mating between a human woman and the entity Yog-Sothoth (or its avatar). Similarly, two Conan stories pit their hero against sorcerers with demonic fathers.

In "The Scarlet Citadel," the wizard Pelias says of his evil rival, Tsotha-lanti:, "[A] dancing-girl of Shadizar slept too near the pre-human ruins on Dagoth Hill and woke in the grip of a black demon; from that unholy union was spawned an accursed hybrid men call Tsotha-Lanti..." (*The Coming of Conan the Cimmerian*, p. 103).

And in "Beyond the Black River," the origin of the Pictish shaman Zogar Sag: "A woman of Gwawela slept in a grove holy to [the Pictish god] Jhebbal Sag. Her babe was Zogar Sag." The association here with "The Dunwich Horror" is even more striking: where the character in Lovecraft's story had a twin brother who "looked more like the father [Yog-Sothoth] than he did" (*The Dunwich Horror and Others*, Arkham House, corrected ninth printing, 1992, p. 198), Zogar Sag has an extraterrestrial half-brother "out of a fire-being of a far realm" (Robert E. Howard, *The Conquering Sword of Conan*: Ballantine Books/Del Rey, 2005, p. 96).

Another Lovecraft-inspired concept appears in the Conan novel, *The Hour of the Dragon*, as Conan is attacked in a nocturnal forest by creatures known as ghouls, "eaters of human flesh, spawn of darkness, children of unholy matings of a lost and forgotten race with the demons of the underworld," who tear at their victims with "dog-like jaws" (see Robert E. Howard, *The Bloody Crown of Conan*, Ballantine Books/Del Rey, 2004, pp. 178, 179). Like the creatures in the Lovecraft-influenced, non-Conan novelette "Dwellers Under the Tomb" discussed previously, the ghouls bear the likeness of the grave-robbing, semi-canine monsters in Lovecraft's "Pickman's Model."

The Conan stories are outside Howard's Cthulhu work, strictly speaking, but they display his ingenuity in absorbing Lovecraft's influence, aligning it with his natural style, and assimilating it with many other stimuli to shape his signature vision of heroic fantasy. "The Lovecraft influence was the final ingredient needed in the rich imaginative mix that produced... Conan the Cimmerian," Howard scholar Rusty Burke has suggested (Rusty Burke, *REH: A Short Biography of Robert E. Howard*: Cross Plains Comics, 1999, p. 53).

PART V
Howard's Defining Additions to the Mythos

This is a listing of the people, places, books, and things that Robert E. Howard devised in stories written intentionally to complement Lovecraft's Cthulhu works. Many of the names were incorporated into the evolving Cthulhu Mythos in subsequent tales by Lovecraft and others. The listing does not include names from Howard stories that were incorporated retroactively by Lovecraft into the Cthulhu framework but were not so intended by Howard at the time of writing (for example, Kathulos from "Skull-Face" and the Serpent Men of Valusia from "The Shadow Kingdom").

BAHADUR, SELIM
Sixteenth-century Turkish scribe and historian, killed in 1526 in the Battle of Schomvaal between the defending Polish-Hungarian forces of Count Boris Vladinoff and the Turkish army of Suleiman the Magnificent during the Turkish invasion of Hungary. Some time before the battle, during a Turkish sweep through the ominous village of Stregiocavar, Selim witnessed and recorded the death of a "monstrous, bloated, wallowing toad-like being" at the hands of the Turks. The soldiers used flames, "ancient steel blessed in old times by Muhammad," and "incantations that were old when Arabia was young" (BN 170). Vladinoff read Selim's account in a parchment in a box taken from the Turk's body. In turn, Vladinoff was killed when cannon-fire destroyed a wall under which he was standing; the falling wall crushed and buried him. The modern-day narrator of "The Black Stone" retrieved Selim's box, and its contents were vital clues in solving the grisly mystery of Stregiocavar (BN).

BLACK BOOK, THE
See NAMELESS CULTS.

BLACK STONE, THE
Howard added two different relics with a common name, the Black Stone, to Mythos lore:

- *The Black Stone of Stregiocavar*: This Black Stone is a tall monolith of mysterious origin that stands on the mountains overlooking Stregiocavar, Hungary. It is octagonal, sixteen feet high, and about a foot-and-a-half thick. The top six-foot length of the monolith is carved with hieroglyphics of no known language. Similar characters were inscribed on the lower ten feet, but these have been partly obliterated by hammering. The inscriptions resemble characters found in carvings and etchings on found in the Yucatan Peninsula of Central America. The "dully gleaming black" material of the monolith has "a curious illusion of transparency" (BN 160). The monolith was the ceremonial site of a prehistoric village called Xuthltan, whose inhabitants were members of a primitive, sadistic witchcraft cult. The cult existed into the sixteenth century, when its practitioners were massacred by invading Turks. Annually during its existence, the cult summoned a toad-like entity from the "Outer Doors" of existence through human sacrifice on Midsummer Eve. The monolith is thought to be the mere spire of a pre-human structure or castle buried underneath the mountains (BN, TR).

- *The Black Stone of the Children of the Night*: The Children of the Night, also called the People of the Dark and the Worms of the Earth, venerated a Black Stone that rested in Dagon's Cave in the British Isles during the early Iron Age and in Dagon's Barrow in the era of Roman Britain. It sat on a pedestal of human skulls. In Dagon's Cave, the pedestal was located behind a black altar on which the Children of the Night offered human sacrifices. In Dagon's Barrow, the heap of skulls itself was the altar. This Black Stone was "a cryptic black object, carven with mysterious hieroglyphics" (PD 153), a "sullen night-black object" (WE 108) compact enough for a man to carry.

BROOLER, PROFESSOR HENDRYK (or HENDRIK)
An anthropologist whose research was known by both Michael Strang and John Stark (HT 147). He also had studied Ketrick, the member of a scholarly circle that included Clemants, Conrad, O'Donnel, Kirowan, and Taveral, and concluded that certain physical attributes of Ketrick suggested atavistic traits (CN 218).

CHILDREN OF THE NIGHT, THE
Also known as the People of the Dark and the Worms of the Earth: a debased culture that preceded the Picts and the Indo-European Celts into the British Isles. They are identified as "Mongoloid" or Asian, but divergent from the genetic type and cultures of historic and modern Asia. Stunted and of "extremely inhuman aspect" (CN 221), these creatures lived underground, preyed on the early Bronze Age tribes of Britain, and were the basis for legends of trolls and dwarves. They venerated the Black Stone, and remnants survived into the Iron Age, the Roman era, and medieval times, with at least one mutated final survivor encountered in the twentieth century. They were able to reproduce with humans, birthing hybrid offspring who bore their traits to greater or lesser degrees. They were associated with locations called Dagon's Cave, Dagon's Barrow, Dagon-moor, Dagon's Ring, and Dagon's Mere, suggesting an undefined relationship with the Cthulhu entity of that name (CN, PD, WE).

CLEMANTS
An associate of Conrad, O'Donnel, Kirowan, and Taveral. He is "a tall, lean man, silent almost to the point of taciturnity," his face lined with the hardships of childhood poverty. He has a dual career as a bestselling author of historical fiction and as editor of *The Cloven Hoof*, "a poetry magazine whose bizarre contents had often aroused the shocked interest of the conservative critics" (CN 220).

CLEMENT, PROFESSOR JAMES
An academician in Richmond, Virginia, with unspecified access to *Nameless Cults*. He provides a copy from which the scholar Tussmann gathers clues about the Temple of the Toad in Honduras (TR).

CONRAD

Four of Howard's Cthulhu stories feature a character named Conrad. They may be the same person or different individuals:

- *Conrad* (no first name) is a scholar whose home in the British Isles houses a fabulous collection of first-edition gothic novels and occult literature, including a copy of *Nameless Cults*. He is an associate of Clemants, O'Donnel, Kirowan, and Taveral. He is versed in obscure lore about the Cthulhu cult and related brotherhoods. He appears in "The Children of the Night" (CN).
- *Conrad* (no first name) visits the ill-regarded Dagon Manor in the unfinished story of that same name (DM).
- *James Conrad* sets off with his friend Kirowan to upstate New York to discover the secret behind the mad poet Justin Geoffrey's sudden change of personality at age ten and the inspiration for the outré imagery in his verse. This occurs in the unfinished story "The House" (TH).
- *John Conrad* and Kirowan witness the ghastly fate of John Grimlan, who sold his soul to powers of darkness in return for extended life, in "Dig Me No Grave" (DG).

In "The Dwellers Under the Tomb," a story associated with but not part of the Mythos, a man named Conrad asks the help of his friend O'Donnel in investigating the apparent return of a man named Jonas Kiles from the dead (DT). Given the identical names, this may be the same Conrad and O'Donnel who meet with other friends to discuss anthropological and occult topics in the "bizarrely fashioned study" of Conrad's home in "The Children of the Night" (CN).

GEOFFREY, JUSTIN

Justin Geoffrey was a poet in the early twentieth century whose published work included *People of the Monolith* and *Out of the Old Land*. He came from a staid family of merchants whose progenitors immigrated from England and settled in New York in 1690. His life was unexceptional up to age ten, when his family visited friends at the foot of the Catskills in New York. Justin wandered off and slept one night in an abandoned house near Old Dutchtown, experiencing bizarre dreams. After that, he began to write poetry of a markedly bizarre and unearthly nature, apparently inspired by his nightmares or visions, earning an underground reputation as a "mad poet." In young adulthood he was extremely thin, with hawkish features. Refusing to attend college, he fled from his family to New York City's Greenwich Village, and first published his verse at age seventeen. He was familiar with and visited the Black Stone of Stregiocavar. He died in an asylum at a young age (BN, TH, TR).

GOL-GOROTH
One of the "ghastly gods and entities" in a catalog that includes Cthulhu, Yog-Sothoth, and Tsathaggua. It was worshipped by a forgotten culture in the lost city of Bal-Sagoth (CN, GS).

GONZALLES, JUAN
A Spanish explorer who appears to have seen but not entered the Temple of the Toad in Honduras in 1793. The indigenous locals told him that the temple harbored "something unusual" (TR).

GRIMLAN, JOHN
A reclusive eccentric and occultist, born John Grymlann on March 10, 1630, in Sussex, England, master there of an estate called Toad's-heath Manor. (Is there an obscure association with the abhorrent Temple of the Toad in Central America? In "The Thing on the Roof," the temple was entered by the scholar Tussmann, who also lived on an estate in Sussex.) Grimlan "gathered as ripe grain the dark secrets of the centuries" and knew of Yog-Sothoth, the cult of Kathulos, and "the noxious winds that blow from Yuggoth" (DG 248). At age 50, he attained to "the dedde citie of Koth" (DG 256) and signed a pact with the entity known as Malik Tous, otherwise known as the Black Master. This agreement granted Grimlan extended life "beyond mortal span." When he died at age 350 on March 10, 1930, he was claimed "[s]oul and body," his corpse borne away by either the "Darke Lord" himself or his avatar in the shape of "a gigantic black shadow like a monstrous bat" (DG 259).

HOODED LAMA, THE
A pretender who tries to incite an uprising in China against Westerners by posing as a priest of the Old Ones (BV).

KARA-SHEHR
"A silent dead city of black stones" located somewhere in the deserts of the Middle East, shunned by the indigenous Bedouins. The name is Turkish for "the Black City"; in Arabic, it is called Beled-el-Djinn, "the City of Devils." In the *Necronomicon*, Abdul Alhazred names it "the City of Evil...the city of the dead on which an ancient curse rested" (FA 20). American Steve Clarney speculates that it originated as an outpost of the ancient Assyrian empire, to which surviving refugees fled after invading Babylonians overran Nineveh, the capital of Assyria. One who came to the Black City from the court of the Assyrian king Asshurbanipal was a sorcerer, Xuthltan, bearing a cursed jewel known as the Fire of Asshurbanipal. The gem's supernatural guardian watches over it from a secret chamber or opening to a cavern in the ruined Temple of Baal.

KETRIC
The sinister manservant of Taverel, the master of Dagon Manor. He is tall and emaciated, with a vulturine cast of features (DM).

KETRICK
A Welsh acquaintance of Clemants, Conrad, Kirowan, O'Donnel, and Taveral, he bears the DNA of the Children of the Night from the long-ago rape of an ancestress. His eyes are "a sort of amber, almost yellow, and slightly oblique" (CN 218). He is also noted for "a slight and occasional lisping of speech." In human heritage, he is descended from a branch of a venerable English Saxon family, the Cedrics, who fled Sussex at the time of the ninth-century Danish invasions and settled in Wales, where they intermarried with English families on the Welsh border.

KIROWAN
There are three Kirowans in Howard's Cthulhu tales. They may be the same man or different individuals:
- In "The Children of the Night," Professor Kirowan is a member of the scholarly fellowship of Clemants, Conrad, Kirowan, O'Donnel, and Taveral who meet at Conrad's home (CN).

- In "Dig Me No Grave," Kirowan (no first name or title) accompanies John Conrad to the house of John Grimlan to carry out Grimlan's request concerning the disposal of his body (DG).
- In "The House," Kirowan (no first name) accompanies James Conrad to New York to investigate the mysterious life of Justin Geoffery (TH).

KOTH

The name "Koth" has two meanings in Howard's Cthulhu stories. Whether the two objects of the name are related, or how they may be related, is uncertain.

One Koth is a "forgotten god" ranked with Cthulhu, Yog-Sothoth, and "all the pre-Adamite Dwellers in the black cities under the sea and the caverns of the earth" (FA 37). The nature, purpose, and appearance of this entity are unknown.

Koth is also the place name of a "dedde citie" in John Grimlan's archaic spelling, in whose "black citadels" lives the Black Master memorialized in humankind's religions under many different names as the source of all evil. Koth, "whereto no mortal hath attained" except John Grimlan, may be located on earth, outer space, or another dimension, for all we are told (DG). It may be that Koth is another name for the Black Master—perhaps his true name as an alien entity—and that the city where he dwells is named for him.

LaDEAU, ALEXIS

A Frenchman who was the closest friend of Von Junzt, the author of *Nameless Cults*. After piecing together and reading the torn scraps of Von Junzt's final manuscript after the German's mysterious death, he burned the pages and cut his own throat (BN).

MAGYAR FOLKLORE

The book *Magyar Folklore* by Dornly (no first name, publisher, or date of publication given) mentions the Black Stone of Stregiocavar, and the belief that anyone who sleeps near the monolith will suffer afterward from terrible nightmares or madness (BN).

NAMELESS CULTS

This is Howard's cornerstone contribution to the Mythos. *Nameless Cults*, published by the occultist Von Junzt in Dusseldorf, Germany, in 1839, is a compendium of material extracted and collated from "countless little-known esoteric books and manuscripts in the original" (BN 153). It mostly addresses cults and sinister objects of worship that existed in Von Junzt's day, according to the author. The original edition of the work is known as the Black Book "because of its dark contents" (TR 162), or under its German title, *Unaussprechlichen Kulten*. It is bound in "heavy leather covers and rusty iron hasps." Pages are now "time-yellowed" with age and use. The contents range from "startling clarity of exposition to murky ambiguity," with "statements and hints to freeze the blood of a thinking man." The ambiguity appears, at least in part, to reflect Von Junzt's reluctance to rigorously transcribe particularly abhorrent or sinister material from his sources. The book is disturbing, nonetheless. Even scholars versed in dark and mortifying matters of the occult regard it as "a book to keep you awake at night" (CN 219).

Other editions besides the original German are flawed. A "cheap and faulty translation" illustrated with woodcuts was published in a pirated edition by Bridewell, some six years after the German edition (London, 1845). This edition is riddled with misspellings and mistranslations. The Golden Goblin Press in New York published "a carefully expurgated edition," deleting a fourth of Von Junzt's original contents, in 1909. This addition was attractively bound, with illustrations by the artist Diego Vasquez; it's unclear whether it drew from Von Junzt's German-language original, Bridewell's English translation, or both. Although Golden Goblin planned to issue the book on the general market, the costs of production became so high that it had to be offered at an expensive and, for most readers, unaffordable price.

Among other subjects dark and dreadful, *Nameless Cults* identifies certain relics from the past as "Keys to Outer Doors—links with an abhorrent past and—who knows?—of abhorrent spheres of the present" (BN 171). Two such "keys" are the Black Stone of Stregiocavar in Hungary and a toad-shaped jewel of doubtful origin in the Temple of the Toad in the jungles of Honduras. The book also treats of the fabulous Pre-Cataclysmic and Hyborian ages, before and after the sinking of Atlantis, and before the beginnings of modern history. Von Junzt also mentions the Picts and describes them in a disputed and apparently erroneous characterization as the culture that gave rise to legends of trolls and goblins.

There may be fewer than a half-dozen copies of the original German imprint still in existence, and they are comparably as hard to find as the tenth-century CE Greek translation of Alhazred's *Necronomicon*. The print run was low, and many people burned their copies after the horrific circumstances of Von Junzt's death in 1840 were circulated. Those known to possess copies are the British scholar Conrad and an American dilettante, Michael Strang. Others who have delved into or are familiar with the book include an American archaeologist named Allison, the explorer Tussmann, and the scholar Taveral. The copy consulted by Tussmann was made available to him with help from an American academician, Professor James Clement. It is unclear whether Clement owned that copy or merely facilitated its purchase or loan from another source (BN, CN, HT, TR, UF).

O'DONNEL

In "The Children of the Night," O'Donnel is one of the guests at a gathering of scholarly acquaintances which includes Clemants, Conrad, Kirowan, and Taverel, at Conrad's home. Struck on the head, he relives an ancient incarnation as a Bronze Age warrior in the British Isles, Aryara. Realizing as a result of the experience that another acquaintance, Ketrick, is partially descended from the malicious Children of the Night, he determines to kill him (CN).

This may or may not be, as well, the O'Donnel in "The Dwellers Under the Tomb," a gun-toting Texan who accompanies a man named Conrad (who may or may not be the same individual as the Conrad in "The Children of the Night") to investigate the Job Kiles mystery. "The Dwellers Under the Tomb" is Lovecraft-influenced but not a Cthulhu story (DT).

O'DONNELL, BLACK JOHN
An adventurer in China who disrupts a plot by a fraudulent priest of the Old Ones to foment an uprising against westerners (BV).

OLD DUTCHTOWN
A venerable town in the New York Catskills that dates from the Dutch colonial era of New York in the seventeenth century. Outside Old Dutchtown stands a deserted old house where ten-year-old Justin Geoffrey slept one night; the rest of his short life was plagued with nightmares and insanity (TH).

REMNANT OF LOST EMPIRES
This was a book written by Otto Dostmann and published by "Das Drachenhaus" Press (Berlin, 1809). *Remnant of Lost Empires* was referenced by Von Junzt in *Nameless Cults* because it mentioned the Black Stone of Hungary. Von Junzt takes exception to Dostmann's claim that the Black Stone was a relic of the Hunnish invasion of Europe under Attila in the fifth century CE, and thus of lesser age than Graeco-Roman ruins in Asia Minor, Dostmann's main interest. Dostmann addresses the hieroglyphics on the Black Stone and says they were Mongoloid in origin, perhaps a determination that he thought bolstered his theory that the monolith was Hunnish. He provides one fact about the Black Stone that *Nameless Cults* doesn't—its location near Stregiocavar, Hungary (BN).

STARK, JOHN
A practitioner of the occult arts who conjures a hoofed, tentacled entity that he keeps hidden in a locked upstairs room in his house in an American town or suburb. He is a powerfully built man who feigns a congenital problem with one leg to cover his excursions at night to procure food for the creature, which grows in size and power as its diet progresses from pet animals to children to adults. Ultimately, Stark is enslaved and then killed by the creature (HT).

STREGIOCAVAR
A village in a remote, mountainous area of Hungary, it does not appear on tourist maps. The name is Slavic for "Witch-Town," referring to its location on the site of a former settlement,

Xuthltan, the home of a now-extinct witchcraft cult. The Black Stone stands on the mountains overlooking the village (BN).

TAVAREL
A taciturn recluse who lives in Dagon Manor (DM).

TAVEREL
An associate of Clemants, Conrad, Kirowan, and O'Donnel in "The Children of the Night." He appears to be familiar with *Nameless Cults*, noting that Von Junzt (mistakenly) had described the Picts as the source for legends of trolls and goblins (CN).

TEMPLE OF THE TOAD, THE
A shine in the remote jungles of Honduras on the Yucatan Peninsula, reared by a forgotten culture more Caucasoid than Indian; some forensic attributes suggest a kinship to a "degraded" culture of lower Egypt. The unknown culture preceded the Indians and went extinct before the arrival of the Spanish. The temple is mentioned in *Nameless Cults*, although the corrupt Bridewell translation mistakenly says that it is located in Guatemala. It is made of basalt, built against a sheer cliff. The columns of the façade are in ruins, the outer walls crumbling, but the inner walls and columns are intact. A chamber inside the temple houses the mummy of the last priest. Around its neck rests an eerie toad-shaped jewel on a chain etched with hieroglyphs that resemble those on the Black Stone in Hungary. The jewel is the key to a crypt beyond, behind a "fantastically carved" door, inhabited by a grisly hoofed entity (BN, TR).

TURKISH WARS
Larson's *Turkish Wars* (no publisher or date given) is a source of information about the death of Count Boris Vladinoff in 1526 (BN).

TUSSMANN
An anthropologist who visited the Temple of the Toad twice, skirting it the first time without having the time and tools to attempt entry. On his second visit, encouraged by an ambiguous reference in *Nameless Cults*, he entered, expecting to find

gold. Instead, he unleashes a supernatural doom that pursues him back to his estate in Sussex (perhaps near John Grimlan's Toad's-heath Manor?) (TR).

UNAUSPRELICHEN KULTEN
See NAMELESS CULTS.

VLADINOFF, COUNT BORIS
A military leader who commanded a small Polish-Hungarian force in a successful skirmish at Schomvaal, Hungary, against an advance guard of the Turkish army during the Ottoman invasion of Europe in 1526. He died after the skirmish when a Turkish bombardment destroyed the wall of an old castle under which he was standing, burying him underneath. Just before his death, he read the manuscript in which Selim Bahadur recorded the destruction of a grisly monster at the Black Stone of Xuthltan (BN).

VON BOEHNK, PROFESSOR
An academician who, as a young student in Vienna in 1880, met John Grimlan (DG).

VON JUNZT
The German author of *Nameless Cults*, born 1795, died 1840. He "spent his entire life...delving into forbidden subjects" and gaining admittance into obscure cults. After the publication of *Nameless Cults*, he spent several months working intently on another manuscript. The contents of that manuscript are unknown. Von Junzt was found in a locked, bolted room with "the marks of taloned fingers" on his throat, the torn fragments of the manuscript scattered around the room. Von Junzt's friend Ladeau re-assembled and read the pages, then burned them and cut his own throat (BN, CN, TR, UF).

XUTHLTAN
Two different "Xuthltans" appear in Howard's Cthulhu stories:
- A place in "The Black Stone." It is "the aboriginal name of the site on which the village [of Stregiocavar) had been built many centuries ago." By association, it may be the name of "a cyclopean black castle," origin unknown, of which the Black Stone is thought to be the merest spire (BN).

- A sorcerer of seventh-century BCE Assyria who fled from Nineveh to the remote border city later named Kara-Shehr and designated by Alhazred as "the City of Evil." Having dared venture into a "nameless vast cavern in a dark, untraveled land," he returned from it with the Fire of Asshurbanipal. This was a mystic red jewel named for the Assyrian king, with which the wizard performed magic and divination. Xuthltan was tortured and put to death by the ruler of Kara-Shehr, who coveted the jewel. Before dying, he placed a curse on the jewel, summoning "a grisly shape" that shriveled the king. The creature still lurks to protect the jewel from further theft by anyone unlucky enough to find Kara-Shehr (FA).

PART VI
Selected Reading List

Readers interested in learning more about Howard's contributions to the Cthulhu Mythos are invited to consult the following works:

BLOSSER, FRED

"The Star Rover and the People of Night." *The Dark Man: The Journal of Robert E. Howard Studies,* ed. Rusty Burke: No. 4: Necronomicon Press, May 1997, pp. 16–18.

CARTER, LIN

"H.P. Lovecraft: The Books." *The Shuttered Room & Other Pieces*, ed. August Derleth: Arkham House, 1959, pp. 212–249.

"H.P. Lovecraft: The Gods." *The Shuttered Room & Other Pieces*, pp. 250–267.

"Nameless Gods and Entities: Robert E. Howard's Contribution to the Cthulhu Mythos." *The Howard Collector*, ed. Glenn Lord: Autumn 1973, pp. 45–52.

CHALKER, JACK LAURENCE

"Howard Phillips Lovecraft: a Bibliography." *The Dark Brotherhood & Other Pieces*, ed. August Derleth: Arkham House, 1966, pp. 198–241.

GRAY, CHARLES O.

"Nameless Cults: History." *The Howard Collector*, ed. Glenn Lord: Ace Books, 1979, pp. 263–265.

HOFFMAN, CHARLES, AND MARC CERASINI

"The Strange Case of Robert Ervin Howard." *The Horror of It All*, ed. Robert M. Price: Borgo Press, 1990, pp. 93–97.

SOLON, BEN

"Howard's Cthuloid Tales." *The Conan Swordbook*, ed. L. Sprague de Camp and George Scithers: The Mirage Press, 1969, pp. 75–80. Also in *The Blade of Conan*, ed. L. Sprague de Camp: Ace Books, 1979, pp. 143–147.

For recent collections of Howard's Cthulhu stories, see *Nameless Cults: The Cthulhu Mythos Fiction of Robert E. Howard*, ed. Robert M. Price: Chaosium Books, 2001, also of interest for Dr. Price's introduction and notes, and *The Horror Stories of Robert E. Howard*, ed. Rusty Burke: Ballantine Books/Del Rey, 2008.

PART VII
Key to Citations

The key to citations of Howard's Cthulhu stories, discussed in Part II, is as follows:

BV: "Black John's Vengeance," in Robert E. Howard, *Tales of Weird Menace*, ed. Rob Roehm: REH Foundation Press, 2010, pp. 131–144.

BN: "The Black Stone," in Robert E. Howard, *Skull-Face Omnibus, Vol. I: Skull-Face and Others*: Panther Books Ltd., 1976, pp. 153–171.

CN: "The Children of the Night," in Robert E. Howard, *Bran Mak Morn, The Last King*, ed. Rusty Burke: Ballantine Books/Del Rey, 2005, pp. 215–232.

DG: "Dig Me No Grave," in Robert E. Howard, *The Dark Man and Others*: Arkham House, 1963, pp. 244–259.

DM: "Dagon Manor," in *The "New" Howard Reader* No. 3, ed. Joe Marek: November 1998, p. 24.

FA: "The Fire of Asshurbanipal," in Robert E. Howard, *Skull-Face Omnibus, Vol. 2: The Valley of the Worm and Others*: Panther Books Ltd., 1976, pp. 18–44.

GS: "The Gods of Bal-Sagoth," in Robert E. Howard, *Swords of the North*, ed. Rob Roehm: REH Foundation Press, 2014, pp. 307–344.

HT: "The Hoofed Thing," in Robert E. Howard, *Trails in Darkness*: Baen Books, 1996, pp. 145–169.

PD: "People of the Dark," in *The Dark Man and Others*, pp. 144–166.

TH: "The House," in *The Howard Reader* No. 8, ed. Joe Marek: August 2003, pp. 19–22.

TR: "The Thing on the Roof," in Robert E. Howard, *The Haunter of the Ring & Other Tales*, ed. M.J. Elliott: Wordsworth Editions Ltd., 2008, pp. 162–170.

UF: "Untitled Fragment" ("Beneath the glare of the sun..."), in *The Howard Collector*, ed. Glenn Lord: Ace Books, 1979, pp. 36–38.

WE: "Worms of the Earth," in *Bran Mak Morn, The Last King*, pp. 83-127; draft version, pp. 249–276.

The key to citations of Howard's Lovecraft-influenced stories outside the Cthulhu cycle, discussed in Part III, is as follows:

CH: "The Cairn on the Headland," in *Skull-Face Omnibus, Vol. I: Skull-Face and Others*, pp. 192–213.

DT: "The Dwellers under the Tomb," in Robert E. Howard, *The Horror Stories of Robert E. Howard*, ed. Rusty Burke: Ballantine Books/Del Rey, 2008, pp. 318–336.

FW: "The Footfalls Within," in Robert E. Howard, *The Savage Tales of Solomon Kane*: Ballantine Books/Del Rey, 2004, pp. 323–345.

NH: "The Noseless Horror," in Robert E. Howard, *Tales of Weird Menace*, ed. Rob Roehm: REH Foundation Press, 2010, pp. 95–110.

APPENDIX A
Kull and the Elder Horrors

The saga of Kull in the chronological order of his life, in mortal combat against foes human and supernatural, was originally outlined in the volume King Kull *(Lancer Books, 1967), edited by the late Glenn Lord. Several stories in that collection (now many decades out of print) were edited or completed by Lin Carter. The citations below are to* Kull: Exile of Atlantis *(Del Rey/Ballantine, 2006), in which all of the stories were returned to the original form in which Howard wrote them.*

Robert E. Howard's Kull of Atlantis, king of primordial Valusia, was the first epic sword-and-sorcery hero of modern literature, the brooding, blade-swinging forerunner of all the intrepid pulp fantasy adventurers who have followed after. With Kull, Howard incorporated the heroism and mystery of ancient myth into a wondrous landscape of forgotten prehistory, haunted by Elder Horrors from other eons and other dimensions.

Howard related Kull's exploits in a rich yet hard-driving prose that remains compulsively readable today, nearly ninety years after the character's introduction in *Weird Tales* magazine. The fantasy-tinged subtexts of the stories reflect psychological and social anxieties that remain with us today—the fear that our enemies, whether real or imagined, are clandestinely conspiring against us; the fear that our lives are directed by inimical, unseen forces beyond our control; the fear that what we regard as "reality" may not be reality at all, but a construct of illusion meant to lull us into complacency, the easier for others to manipulate and harm us.

Thanks to the gripping nature of Howard's concepts, characterizations, and writing style, Kull was an instant favorite among fans. Some aficionados have rated him even above Conan as Howard's towering achievement in fantastic literature.

H.P. Lovecraft said:

> Mr. Howard began in 1929—with "The Shadow Kingdom," in the August *Weird Tales*—that succession of tales of the prehistoric world for which he soon grew so famous. The earlier specimens described a very distant age in man's history—when Atlantis, Lemuria, and Mu were above the waves, and when the shadows of pre-human reptile men rested upon the primal scene.

Lovecraft was so impressed that he added a major element from the Kull saga to his fabled Cthulhu Mythos.

August W. Derleth stated:

> In the tales concerning Solomon Kane, Bran Mak Morn, Kull, and Conan, there is quite possibly more blood-letting and more lusty carnage than in any other group of stories which appeared in pulp magazines in America during the 1930s. ... It will be observed by the alert reader that...the earlier Howard wrote more skillfully than the Howard who created and exploited the popular Conan.

In Howard's imagined prehistory, Kull lived, warred, and ruled in the Pre-Cataclysmic Age of more than 100,000 years. The continents of Atlantis and Lemuria had not yet disappeared beneath the sea, nor the islands of the Picts, whose rough-hewn culture stretched even further back into the distant past, to times immemorial. The Atlanteans, Lemurians, and Picts were the barbarians of that time. Their civilized but increasingly degenerate contemporaries were the folk who populated the Seven Empires of the mainland, or Thurian, continent. These Seven Empires were Kamelia, Verulia, Grondar, Zarfhaana, Thule, Commoria, and Valusia (the most splendid of the seven). To the distant east, the known world ended at the River Stagus, the dim memory of which persists in our legends of the Styx, the River of Death.

APPENDIX A: KULL AND THE ELDER HORRORS

In even more distant prehistory, the original masters of the Younger Earth were abhorrent, inhuman horrors—"grisly beings of the Elder Universe" (KA 35) such as the wolf-people, the bat-people, and most fearsome of all, the snake-people. Emerging as a dominant species, the human race vanquished these devils and elevated the god Valka as its chosen deity. Yet the shadow of the snake-people continued to brood over the Seven Empires. As humans forgot the old wars against these children of darkness, "the Things returned in crafty guise" (KA 36). Lurking as the priests of the powerful Serpent Cult and able to assume human semblance, the snake-people were the hidden masters of Valusia, controlling a succession of puppet dynasties and sometimes, in human guise, supplanting the very kings themselves. Then came Kull...

"Exile of Atlantis"
Originally published in King Kull, *Lancer Books: 1967*

This short story reveals the origins of King Kull as a youth in barbaric Atlantis. An orphan of unknown parentage, he had been reared in the wild by tigers and wolves before finding a home in the Sea-mountain Tribe. Thus, he is a man of savage beginnings like Rudyard Kipling's Mowgli, Edgar Rice Burroughs' Tarzan, Otis Adelbert Kline's Tam, and Leigh Brackett's Eric John Stark. In a dream or premonition, he sees himself as the king of a great empire. Then, with a flint dagger, he grants a swift and merciful death to a young woman about to be burned alive for transgressing the laws of her tribe: she had married a Lemurian pirate, the hereditary enemy of Atlantis. Kull dives into the ocean to escape the wrath of his fellows.

"The Shadow Kingdom"
Originally published in Weird Tales, *August 1929*

Long after his flight from Atlantis, Kull has realized his boyhood dream (or his glimpse of the future). Riding a tide of unrest in Valusia, he has seized the throne of that ancient nation and has been crowned King Kull. His tribulations have only begun. The hereditary nobility schemes to displace him, and some in the populace grumble against him because they resent being ruled by a barbarian. Most daunting of all, he learns from the Pictish ambassador Ka-nu and the Pictish warrior Brule the Spear-slayer that the mysterious Serpent-people still lurk in the shadows and plan his assassination. The conspiracy plunges him into a paranoiac nightmare as the creatures pose, successively, as his councilor Tu, his personal bodyguard of Red Slayers, Brule the Pict, and even as Kull himself. With blades and bravery, Kull and Brule expose the plot and vanquish the pretenders, and Kull pledges to eradicate the Serpent People for good.

This story contains the fullest and most detailed history and descriptions of the snake-men. These loathsome beings can be slain by sword and spear, as humans are slain. After death, a serpent man's powers of illusion are dissipated, and it assumes its true form as a manlike being with "the head of a mighty snake" (KA 45). The saga of Kull suggests that he succeeded in smashing the power of the serpent men, but it does not explicitly demonstrate that he wiped out all of the ophidian breed, as he pledged to do. H.P. Lovecraft incorporated them into the lore of the Cthulhu Mythos, where they are remembered as "the reptile people of fabled Valusia" (see "The Shadow out of Time," in *The Dreams in the Witch House and Other Weird Stories*, ed. S.T. Joshi: Penguin Books, 2004, p. 359).

"The Altar and the Scorpion"
Originally published in King Kull

A distant Valusian city shudders under the influence of another Elder Horror, the cult of the enigmatic Black Shadow. The Black Shadow is the symbol of the hideous Unnamable One, one of "the real gods, the powerful, the terrible gods, who came from forgotten worlds and lost realms of blackness," born "on frozen stars, and black stars brooding beyond the light of any star" (KA 137). As Kull (offstage) sets forth to eradicate the cult, the archpriest of the Black Shadow, Thuron, prepares to sacrifice a young couple. The boy calls on his own deity, the Scorpion, to rescue him and his sweetheart.

APPENDIX A: KULL AND THE ELDER HORRORS

"The Cat and the Skull"
Originally published in King Kull *as "Delcardes' Cat"*

The beautiful courtesan Delcardes owns Saremes, a cat that apparently can think and talk like a human, but with an added gift of clairvoyance. A warning from Saremes sends Kull to the Forbidden Lake where he encounters an apparently trans-dimensional underwater world of sea-serpents, shark men, and a mysterious lost race. Kull learns that the quest was instigated by a sorcerer, Thulsa Doom, whose face "was a bare white skull, in whose eye sockets flamed livid fire" (KA 114). He is "a satellite of the great serpent" (the awful god of the Serpent People), and a daunting figure in his own right: "an owner of magic black and unholy, with "the gift of illusion and of invisibility" (KA 115). Having been slain once, he claims that he can never be killed again as a mortal human may be killed. Howard's character was re-imagined and re-purposed as the wizardly leader of a snake cult in Conan the Cimmerian's time in the movie *Conan the Barbarian* (1982), as portrayed by James Earl Jones.

"The Screaming Skull of Silence"
Originally published in King Kull *as "The Skull of Silence"*

On the Day of the King's Fear, Kull finds his legendary courage tested as he journeys to the Skull of Silence, an isolated keep in mountainous Zalgara. There, legends say, the ancient sage Raama imprisoned the essence of complete silence. Breaching the fortress, the king unwittingly releases "a thing, elemental and real," a complete absence of sound—an "onslaught of cosmic forces...hotter than flame and colder than ice" (KA 125). Only Kull's bravery and the aid of a wizard's gong save the world from inundation by utter, brain-shattering silence. Perhaps the most surprising and unconventional Elder Horror in the series.

"By This Axe I Rule!"
Originally published in King Kull

This is a tale of action and philosophy in which sorcerers and serpent men are apparently on a rare sabbatical. Kull survives a conspiracy against his life and, wielding a battle-axe, shatters the ancient stone tablet on which the Valusian law of slavery is carved. "I am the law!" Kull declares (KA 179). He will uphold just laws and eliminate the unjust.

"The Striking of the Gong"
Originally published in King Kull

Struck down by a would-be assassin and hearing the reverberation of a palace gong before he falls unconscious, Kull finds himself on the threshold of eternity. There are no Elder Horrors in this tale, only an odyssey of wonder in which Kull "travel[s] the longest journey of [his] life, and...live[s] countless millions of years during the striking of the gong" (KA 132).

"Swords of the Purple Kingdom"
Originally published in King Kull

Like "By This Axe I Rule!", this is a tale of action and intrigue as Howard again shifts from the realms of horror and metaphysics to swashbuckling adventure. Another conspiracy, this one directed by a mastermind known as the Masked One in collusion with the rival nation of Verulia, threatens to topple Kull. It culminates in the bloody Battle of the Stair, in which Kull is besieged by more than 20 frenzied swordsmen.

"The Mirrors of Tuzun Thune"
Originally published in Weird Tales, *September 1929*

In his House of a Thousand Mirrors, the mystical Tuzun Thune, a "wizard of the Elder Race" (KA 55), holds "the secrets of life and death." Restlessly seeking to satisfy a "longing beyond life's longings," Kull travels there at the suggestion of a courtesan. In the wizard's mirrors, the king views worlds beyond his, and wonders: Who is the real Kull? He, or the reflection in the glass? Brule's intervention saves the king from a bizarre doom.

"The King and the Oak"
Originally published in Weird Tales, *February 1939*

An eerie, miniature epic in verse. Riding alone through a spectral forest, Kull finds himself trapped by the ancient oaks who were "the lords ere man had come, and shall be lords again" (KA 213). Whether the interlude was a dream, a prophecy, or an encounter with another forgotten life-form pre-dating humankind, Howard leaves Kull and the reader to decide. Fantasy enthusiasts may be reminded of J.R.R. Tolkien's Ents from *Lord of the Rings*, and of the living tree on the planet Jupiter that nearly devours John Carter in Edgar Rice Burroughs' "Skeleton Men of Jupiter."

"The Curse of the Golden Skull"
Originally published in The Howard Collector, *Spring 1967*

This story contains a veritable catalog of evocative and sinister names apparently denoting a mix of deities, Elder Horrors, and infernal texts: "Hotath and Helgor...Ra and Ka and Valka...Vramma and Jaggta-noga and Kamma and Kulthas...the fane of the Black Gods, the tracks of the Serpent Ones, the talons of the Ape Lords and the iron bound books of Shuma Gorath" (KA 141). In his mountaintop temple, the wizard Rotath lies dying from a sword-wound inflicted by "the barbarian chief, Kull of Atlantis," apparently at the instigation of the king of Lemuria. Rotath evokes the litany in placing a malediction on his own bones, so that they will bring doom to others one day. He seals the curse with a spell to ensure that his skull and skeleton will survive the passage of time. The sinking of Lemuria reduces the mountain to a small, swampy island to which—in our day—an explorer travels. There, he finds that Rotath's curse lives on in the wizard's skull and skeleton, fantastically and accursedly transmuted into gold.

"Kings of the Night"
Originally published in Weird Tales, *November 1930*

Pictish sorcery draws Kull into our own historical era of Imperial Rome, to help the Pictish King Bran Mak Morn resist an invasion by the Roman Legions. There are no Elder Horrors in this tale, only the wonderment with which Kull reflects on the incident as a dream in which he went into "a far clime and a far time...and fought for the king of a strange shadow-people" (KA 244).

Sadly, three Kull stories survive in Howard's pure-text form only as incomplete fragments:

"The Black City"
Originally published pure-text in Kull, *Bantam Books: 1978*

On a rare vacation in the Valusian pleasure city of Kamula, Kull is drawn into action when one of his Pictish entourage goes missing and another is found foully murdered. He and Brule discover a hidden panel, from behind which issues "a thin, wailing sound as of a ghostly piping." The piping contains "all the hate and venom of a thousand demons" (KA 149). One wonders what crawling horrors would have been revealed had Howard finished the story.

"Untitled Fragment" ("'Thus,' said Tu, chief councilor...")
Originally published pure-text in Kull, *Bantam Books: 1978*

Kull, Brule, and the king's bodyguard, the Red Slayers, pursue when Lala-ah, a Valusian noblewoman, elopes with a foreign adventurer, Felgar, to escape an unpleasant arranged marriage. Kull is angered by an insulting message from Felgar. The trail leads far to the east, to the end of the known world, where Kull meets Karon the ferryman,"a man of the Elder Race,who ruled the world before Valusia was" (KA 84). Beyond the river Stagus where Karon plies his boat lie "[n]ameless horrors and... ghastly shapes of doom" (KA 84). Alas, the fragment ends before the reader is introduced to these monsters or demons, and before Kull can measure his sword against them.

"Untitled Fragment" ("Three men sat at a table...")

Originally published pure-text in Kull, *Bantam Books: 1978*

As Brule, Kull, and Prince Ronaro sit over a game of chess, Kull stakes his wizard-piece against Brule's warrior-piece. Brule begins to relate an adventure that occurred in his youth, on his first raid, when his life "hung on the balance of power between a Pictland wizard and me" (KA 153). One wishes that Howard had completed the story, in which another potent man of magic undoubtedly would have appeared.

So ended the epic of Kull with its heroes and horrors, to be followed in two years' time by the mighty Conan.

APPENDIX B

An Argument of Dates in the Life of Solomon Kane, Foe of Demons and Dastards

Solomon Kane, Robert E. Howard's grim avenging Puritan swordsman in the era of Queen Elizabeth I, was highly regarded by H.P. Lovecraft.

The creator of dread Cthulhu and the frightful *Necronomicon* wrote:

> With these tales [of Solomon Kane] Mr. Howard struck what proved to be one of his most effective accomplishments—the description of vast megalithic cities of the elder world, around whose dark towers and labyrinthine nether vaults clings an aura of pre-human fear and necromancy which no other writer could duplicate. These tales also marked Mr. Howard's development of that skill and zest in depicting sanguinary conflict which became so typical of his work" (*The Savage Tales of Solomon Kane*, Ballantine Books/Del Rey, 2004, pp. xiii–xiv).

In his observation about "vast megalithic cities of the elder world" in association with the Solomon Kane fantasies, Lovecraft may have had in mind the vast African complex of Negari in "The Moon of Skulls" and "the silent city of stone" (*The Savage Tales of Solomon Kane*, p. 236) in "The Hills of the Dead." Negari with its mad queen and "gray halls of death and decay" (*The Savage Tales of Solomon Kane*, p. 113) is the last outpost of sunken Atlantis. The nameless ruined city in the other story is a den of savage vampires. Lovecraft himself fantasized a forgotten Congo city ruled by a "white ape-goddess" (*The Call of Cthulhu and Other Weird Stories*, ed. S.T. Joshi: Penguin Books, 1999, p. 19). This fancy appeared in an early story, "Facts Concerning the Late Arthur Jermyn and His Family," also published as "Arthur Jermyn" and "The White Ape." Had Lovecraft and Howard thought to collaborate on a story about an unrecorded journey by Solomon Kane to Lovecraft's Onga country, what an adventure that would have been.

Howard fans widely agree with Lovecraft that Kane is a towering creation whose adventures in lands of sword and sorcery set the stage for King Kull and Conan. But enthusiasts debate, almost as strongly, the internal chronology of the series. Which story preceded or followed another, according to where each would have fallen in the course of Kane's life? In what year did a particular story take place? Few explicit clues exist in the Kane saga with which to answer those questions. The implicit clues are often confusing and contradictory.

I would begin a Kane chronology with these dates:

- **1530**: Solomon Kane is born in Devonshire, England.
- **1553**: The events in "Skulls in the Stars" and "The Right Hand of Doom," where Kane encounters supernatural horrors in rural England.

These and other proposed dates in the timeline that follows are based largely on my extrapolations from the late Glenn Lord's pioneering work. Mr. Lord was the first to arrange the Solomon Kane stories according to a consistent internal chronological order, in *Red Shadows* (West Kingston, RI: Donald M. Grant, 1968). We fans who first began to read Howard in the 1960s will find it hard to believe that *Red Shadows* observes its 50th anniversary this year. Subsequent editors followed the same chronology in compiling the collections *Skulls in the Stars* and *Hills of the Dead* (Bantam Books, 1978 and 1979), *Solomon Kane* (Baen Books, 1995), and *The Savage Tales of Solomon Kane* (Wandering Star Books, 1998; Ballantine Books/Del Rey, 2004).

APPENDIX B: SOLOMON KANE

Mr. Lord suggested that "[t]he events in 'Skulls in the Stars' probably occurred no later than 1560." He proposed "Skulls in the Stars" and "The Right Hand of Doom" as the earliest of Kane's adventures: "Kane obviously was a young man when we first meet him" in these stories (*Red Shadows*, p. 11).

In some of the later stories (that is, later chronologically, as the recorded events in Kane's life were placed in relation to one another by Mr. Lord), Howard alludes to a setting during the reign of Queen Elizabeth I, 1558–1603. For example, see "Hawk of Basti," *Savage Tales of Solomon Kane*, p. 259. However, in "The Right Hand of Doom," reference is made to "the king's soldiers" (*Savage Tales of Solomon Kane*, p. 21).

Only two kings of England would fit comfortably into a timeframe in which Kane was in the prime of his life during the Elizabethan era: King Edward VI (ruled 1547–53) and King James I (ruled 1603–25). Given Mr. Lord's chronology, the reference would have to apply to Edward, so any date for these first two stories later than 1553 would be impossible.

As Mr. Lord notes (*Red Shadows*, p. 11), Kane has already "gained renown for his deeds in unrecorded adventures." See "The Right Hand of Doom," in which a character calls Kane "dangerouser than a wolf" (*Savage Tales of Solomon Kane*, p. 22). This argues for Kane to be old enough to have already established a reputation, yet not so old that indisputably he would be past his years of vitality in later stories. An age of 23 is a reasonable guess.

- **1562–63**: Kane serves as a captain in the French army during the religious wars between Protestants and Catholics in France.
- **1564–65**: The events in "Red Shadows"; "Rattle of Bones"; "Death's Black Riders"; and "The Castle of the Devil."

In "Red Shadows," the scene of Kane's adventures shifts from England to continental Europe. Mr. Lord proposes (*Red Shadows*, p. 37) that the story follows a period of military service in France during the religious wars between Catholics and Protestants. This suggestion apparently is based on a reference in a later story, "The Blue Flame of Vengeance" (*Savage Tales of Solomon Kane*, p. 187). The first of the French religious wars of the 16th century occurred in 1562 and 1563. The events in "Red Shadows" lead Kane to Africa, whence he returns to Europe and travels through Germany's Black Forest for a time.

- **1566-69**: Kane sails with another adventurer, John Silent, to fight the Turkish corsairs. He is captured by the pirates and spends time as a galley slave before escaping. A later story alludes to Kane's Turkish captivity (*Savage Tales of Solomon Kane*, p. 278). Mr. Lord proposes that this phase of Kane's life followed his meeting with John Silent in "The Castle of the Devil" who, when Kane meets him, is on his way to sail against the Turks (*Savage Tales of Solomon Kane*, p. 88).
- **1571–73**: Kane participates in Sir Francis Drake's voyages to the Caribbean and the New World, where he gains experience in fighting the native Indians of Darien and learning their woodcraft (*Savage Tales of Solomon Kane*, p. 326).
- **1574–76**: In "The Moon of Skulls" (Kane's second journey into Africa), Kane slays Sir John Taferal in a duel; he travels to the Mediterranean and into Africa to find Taferal's kidnapped niece.
- **1577–79**: Kane again sails with Drake; he is present during the execution of Sir Thomas Doughty in 1578 ("The One Black Stain"). The sketchy history of Kane's life records that Drake praised Kane as "Devon's king of swords" (*Savage Tales of Solomon Kane*, p. 278).
- **1581–83**: The events in "The Blue Flame of Vengeance" (in England again).
- **1585–86**: Kane may have accompanied his friend Sir Richard Grenville on Grenville's expedition to the North American coast, in what is now North Carolina. See a reference to Kane having "battled red Indians in the New Lands," *Savage Tales of Solomon Kane*, p. 278. To be candid, this entry in the chronology is even more speculative than others, and assumes that the reference was not associated instead with Kane's experiences with the Central American natives of Darien, which I noted previously. Still, Kane's warm reference to Grenville as

APPENDIX B: SOLOMON KANE 103

a "friend of old times" on later occasion (*Savage Tales of Solomon Kane*, p. 271) suggests a long-standing closeness between the two men.

- **1591**: Kane sails with Grenville to plunder the Spanish fleet bringing treasure home from the New World. Grenville's ship, the *Revenge*, is overwhelmed by the Spaniards, Grenville dies in battle, and Kane is imprisoned by the Inquisition in Spain.

See the reference to Kane's service with Grenville in 1591 in *Savage Tales of Solomon Kane*, pp. 381–382.

- **1593–?**: The events in "The Hills of the Dead," "Hawk of Basti," "The Return of Sir Richard Grenville, " "Wings in the Night," "The Footfalls Within," and "The Children of Asshur."

The time frame for Kane's third journey into Africa is extremely uncertain. This was the journey in which Kane encountered a monstrous Elder Horror that may have been kin to the primordial entities of Lovecraft: "a gigantic pulsing red Thing that had neither shape nor earthly substance" (*Savage Tales of Solomon Kane*, p. 342).

Given a presumed birth date of 1530 for Kane, and given Kane's association with recorded adventures involving Drake in 1578 and Grenville in 1591, the earlier stories can be fitted into a loose but serviceable chronology. After 1591, lacking a similar historical frame of reference, pure speculation comes into play.

If we presume that Kane was in his sixties by this time, some may question whether a man of that age would have the stamina and strength to undergo the arduous and physically challenging adventures described in these stories, including fierce hand-to-hand combat with vampires and winged harpies. On the other hand, why should we assume that Howard's extraordinary heroes were subject to the same infirmities and ravages of age as we average humans?

- **1610**: The events in "Solomon Kane's Homecoming."

This date for Kane's last recorded appearance was suggested by Mr. Lord under the assumption that a certain "Bess" who is named in the poem, and who "in the quiet churchyard by the sea...has slept these seven years," was Queen Elizabeth I, who died in 1603. Given Kane's stated antipathy to the Tudor dynasty (*Savage Tales of Solomon Kane*, p. 259), some observers have questioned whether a reference to Queen Elizabeth indeed was intended, thus leaving the date of "Solomon Kane's Homecoming" open to question (see Ramsey Campbell, "Introduction," in *Solomon Kane*, Baen Books, 1995, pp. 4–5). Still, there is no counter-evidence for a different date; until such evidence presents itself, 1610 is as good a date as any other.

I should again note that the arrangement of stories, above, derives from the work of Glenn Lord, but it in no way is intended to imply that Mr. Lord would have concurred with my extrapolations about the dates represented by the tales. My notes reflect ideas and suggestions shared with me by Rusty Burke and Roy Thomas, but any error of historical fact, interpretation, and extrapolation are entirely my own. Other Howard aficionados have proposed different theories about Solomon Kane's timeline, all arguably as valid as mine. It's part of the fun in reading Howard that so many aspects of his stories are ripe for literary sleuthing. May the game continue forever!

APPENDIX C
Horrors from the Deep: Howard's Stories of Haunted Seaports

H.P. Lovecraft's stories about Innsmouth, Kingsport, and other imaginary, horror-haunted villages on the New England coast are classic. The old ports of Massachusetts and Rhode Island held an alluring charm for Lovecraft. He knew them first-hand and liked to use them as settings for fantasies about witchcraft and incursions by the Elder Horrors of the Cthulhu Mythos.

Lovecraft's friend and colleague Robert E. Howard, living in landlocked west-central Texas, only rarely used coastal settings as a backdrop for horror. When he wrote his own stories in the Cthulhu Mythos, their dire doings usually occurred inland, on lonely moors in Great Britain or in the fearful mountains of Hungary. Outside the Mythos, Howard experimented with three stories about the supernatural on wind-lashed docks and beaches. Written before Howard began to correspond with Lovecraft and started to incorporate HPL's themes and style into his own horror fiction, the stories are minor ones in REH's body of work. Nevertheless, like all of Howard's tales, they invite reading and analysis.

In "Sea Curse" (*Weird Tales*, May 1928), set in the fishing village of Faring Town, the young niece of old Moll Farrell is seduced and discarded by the swaggering bully John Kulrek. In shame, the girl drowns herself. Moll, reputed to be a witch, places "the curse of the Foul Fiend" on Kulrek and "set[s] the seal of death" on his crony, Lie-lip Canool (*Eons of the Night*:

Baen Books, 1996, p. 184). They will be the death of each other, the old woman swears.

Moll tells Kulrek that he will "die in horror far out upon the cold gray sea," and before the end of summer, "your corpse will lie at my feet." The imprecation comes to pass months later. Lie-lip returns from a long voyage without Kulrek. And then an eerie, decaying galley appears off the village in a dense bank of fog.

Where does Faring Town reside? In New England, Newfoundland, Great Britain, Greenland, or elsewhere? Howard doesn't say. "From the names of the people and the climate, it might have lain on the coasts of Maine, or County Donegal, or the Yorkshire Strands," author S.M. Stirling notes in his short introduction to the story in the collection *Eons of the Night* (p. 181).

Some have suggested that the names Kulrek and Lie-lip have a ring of Jack London's northland stories to them—"if indeed the Faring Town tales may be said to owe something to Howard's favorite writer," Rusty Burke writes (Introduction to *The Horror Stories of Robert E. Howard*: Ballantine Books/Del Rey, 2008, p. xix). In devising the wonderful name Lie-lip, Howard may have remembered, perhaps unconsciously, the name of the wolf Lip-lip in London's *White Fang*.

If the village is imprecisely defined in a geographical sense, its taverns and wharfs nevertheless have an impressionistic vividness, washed with "the cold gray tides [that] came sweeping along the bleak strands, bearing the rain and sleet of the sharp east breezes" (*Eons of the Night*, p. 185). Moll Farrell, "a grim, gaunt old dame" (p. 183), has the same elemental presence. She calls out the brutal Kulrek and Lie-lip as none of the men in the village ever dared to do, because "all feared them" (p. 182). One wonders whether she represented Howard's boyhood memories of his grandmother, whom he described in similarly formidable terms to Lovecraft: "All the gloominess and dark mysticism of the Gaelic nature was hers, and there was no light and mirth in her" (*Robert E. Howard: Selected Letters, 1923–1930*, p. 59).

Kulrek and Lie-lip, "the brawlers and braggarts, the loud boasters and hard drinkers of Faring Town" (*Eons of the Night*, p. 181), are the dark reverse-image twins of Howard's roistering heroes Conan and Wild Bill Clanton. One can visualize them as the spitting images of Wallace Beery's Long John Silver from the 1934 movie *Treasure Island* and John Barrymore's swaggering Ahab Ceely in the unlikely 1930 film adaptation of *Moby Dick*. Were they drawn from young Bob Howard's memories or impressions of the oil-field roughnecks who had flocked to Cross Plains, Texas, in the oil-boom days?

The horror element of the story, when it materializes toward the end, isn't likely to seem scary to readers, especially those who are accustomed to similar imagery in the Pirates of the Caribbean movies. Nevertheless, the way in which old Moll's curse is realized has a fine flavor of fantasy.

Faring Town returns in "Out of the Deep," unsold during Howard's lifetime but eventually published in *Magazine of Horror*, November 1967. The drowned body of young Adam Falcon washes up on the beach, strangely covered with a type of seaweed only found at the bottom of the ocean. Adam's sweetheart Margaret is killed that night while sitting with the body. The corpse disappears. One of Margaret's rejected suitors, John Gower, is suspected of her murder and placed in the village stocks to await trial.

Then Gower himself and other townsfolk are killed. One witness claims that the murderer was the dead man, Adam Falcon. The unnamed narrator of the story, apparently not the same person as the seemingly much younger narrator of "Sea Curse," suspects the truth that lurks behind the mystery of the killings. As the other villagers hide themselves away behind locked doors, he goes down to the beach to confront a "horror that has come upon Earth of yore—so long ago that all men have forgotten the tales; all except such as I, whom men name fool" (*Eons of the Night*, p. 199).

The narrator says he is "considered strange and foolish" by others in Faring Town (p. 199). In this he seems to mirror Howard's own feelings of being an outsider in his home town, as described by E. Hoffman Price in his memoir of Howard and as Howard himself suggested through his surrogate, the young narrator of the fictionalized, dramatized roman à clef, *Post Oaks and Sand Roughs*. Like the moor ghost whom Solomon Kane confronts in "Skulls in the Stars," the horrific visitant in "Out of the Deep" seems invincible when its victims are frozen in terror, but as the narrator says in the reckoning on the beach, it "may be slain by a man who does not fear you."

The narrator solves the murders by studying the circumstances of the killings and the testimony of witnesses (Howard plays fair by providing clues throughout the story) and sifting them through his knowledge of ancient lore. He also seems to have the advantages of a psychic linkage with the sea itself, a mystical insight into its secrets, and a contradictory sense that natural forces like the ocean simultaneously exist beyond human understanding and emotion, yet have their own capricious whims. "I have no part of man," the narrator hears in the wash of the tides. This sentiment seems to correspond to the central tenet that informs the fiction of Howard's colleague, Lovecraft: "that common human laws and interests and emotions have no validity or significance in the vast cosmos-at-large" (*The Call of Cthulhu and Other Weird Stories*, ed. S.T. Joshi: Penguin Books, 1999, p. xvi).

And yet the story also suggests that nature may be sentient and even cruelly perverse, as the narrator reflects on the factors that inspired his theory about the evil besetting Faring Town: "Mayhap the sea, strange and fickle even to her chosen, had whispered something to my inner mind, had betrayed her own" (*Eons of the Night*, p. 198). Where Lovecraft's protagonists typically run away when horror presents itself, the narrator of "Out of the Deep" chooses to meet it head-on, as Howard's characters usually do. As Howard readers might expect, the final confrontation resolves into physical combat.

The historical setting of Faring Town is as uncertain as its geographical setting. References to "ships...still in use among the heathens of Barbary" (p. 188) and to stocks as a form of temporary incarceration (p. 196) suggest a late eighteenth- or early nineteenth-century time-frame.

The locale of a third story about horrors in a seaside village, one apparently unrelated to Faring Town, is better defined. "Restless Waters" (first published in *Witchcraft & Sorcery* No. 10, 1974) takes place on the New England coast in 1845. The narrator is the serving boy at the local taproom, the Silver Slipper.

One character in the tale is named John Gower, but there's no indication that he's the same Gower who appears in "Out of the Deep." In the Silver Slipper on a stormy night, conversation reveals that short-tempered Captain Starkey is about to betroth his niece and ward, Betty, to an older merchant, Harmer. Starkey stands to benefit financially from the marriage. Betty still pines for her sweetheart Dick Hansen, missing and thought drowned. Starkey is regarded as a hard man because he hanged his first mate, Tom Siler, for mutiny.

As tempers grow short from too much strong drink, attorney Jonas Hopkins reveals that Hansen's disappearance and Siler's hanging were linked by a common motive having to do with Starkey's plan to unite his niece in an unwilling marriage to Harmer. The noise of the gale at the window startles the young narrator: "an unearthly coldness stole over me, as if through a suddenly opened door, a wind from some other sphere had breathed upon me" (*The Gods of Bal-Sagoth*: Ace Books, 1979, p. 176). Ghostly vengeance ensues, although—as in many classic ghost stories—it's implied that the spectral visitation in the denouement of "Restless Waters" may just as easily have a natural explanation...for the young narrator, an illusion brought on by the stormy night and heightened emotion; for another character, an outcome of drunken rage.

Read as Howard's bid to write a traditional ghost story somewhat in the manner of J. Sheridan Le Fanu and other nineteenth-century practitioners, it isn't a bad tale. Clearly, though, it didn't play to Howard's greater strengths in writing blood-and-thunder adventure and horror. Plenty of *Weird Tales* regulars could turn out readable ghost stories, including August Derleth, Mary Elizabeth Counselman, and Seabury Quinn, but in his area of specialty, there was only one Robert E. Howard.

About the Author

Fred Blosser is a long-time enthusiast of Robert E. Howard. His articles, critiques, and observations about Howard and his work appeared in the Marvel Comics magazines *The Savage Sword of Conan*, *The Conan Saga*, and *Kull and the Barbarians*, as well as in the semi-professional journals *The Howard Collector*, *The Howard Review*, *The Dark Man*, and *Cross Plains*. He has also appeared in *Cinema Retro*, *Amra*, *Crypt of Cthulhu*, *The Dark Side*, *Savage Tales*, *Mystery Scene*, and *The Armchair Detective*.

He is the author of the "Informal Guide to Robert E. Howard" series of scholarly works, which currently include this volume and its follow-up, *Western Weirdness and Voodoo Vengeance*, as well as *Savage Scrolls: Volume 1*, all from Pulp Hero Press.

About the Author

Made in the USA
Monee, IL
11 April 2025